PIANO · VOCAL · GUITAR

Solid Gold Hits

T0087320

ISBN 978-1-4234-0035-6

7777 W. BLUEMOUND RD. P.O. BOX 13819 MILWAUKEE, WI 53213

Visit Hal Leonard Online at
www.halleonard.com

CONTENTS

SO WHAT'CHA WANT

Words and Music by MICHAEL DIAMOND,
ADAM HOROVITZ and ADAM YAUCH

Heavily

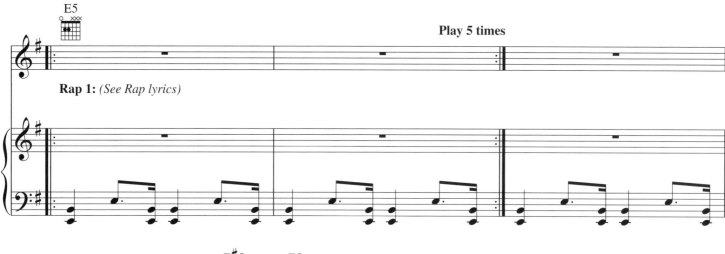

Play 5 times

Rap 1: (See Rap lyrics)

So what-'cha, what-'cha, what-'cha want? What-'cha want?__ And you're so

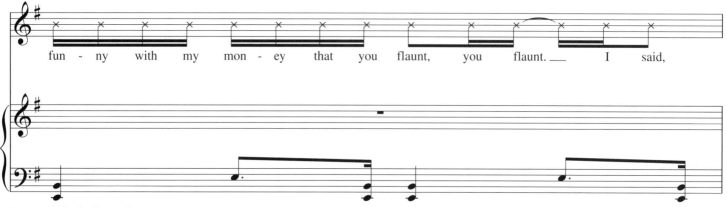

fun-ny with my mon-ey that you flaunt, you flaunt.__ I said,

*Recorded a half step lower.

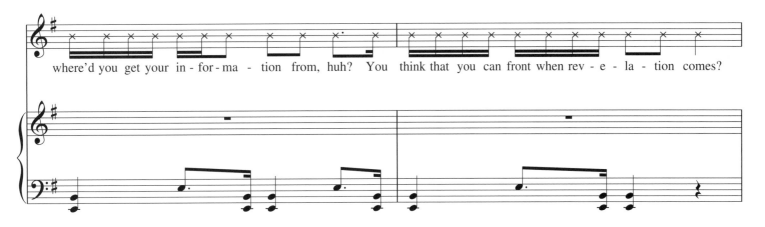

where'd you get your in-for-ma-tion from, huh? You think that you can front when rev-e-la-tion comes?

Yeah, you can't front on that.

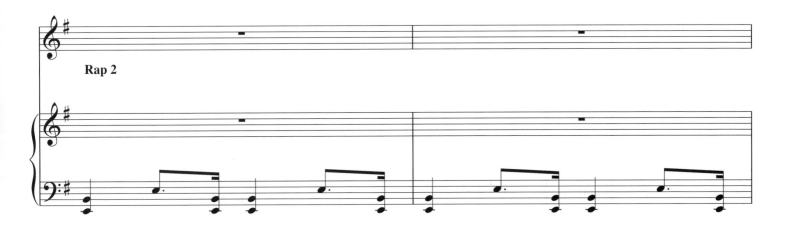

Rap 2

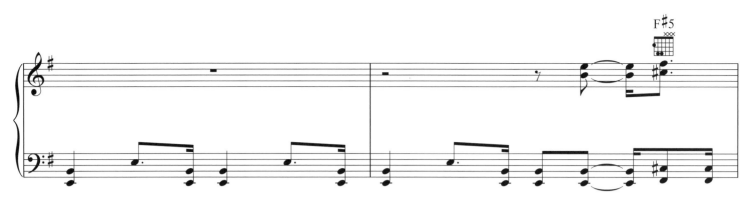

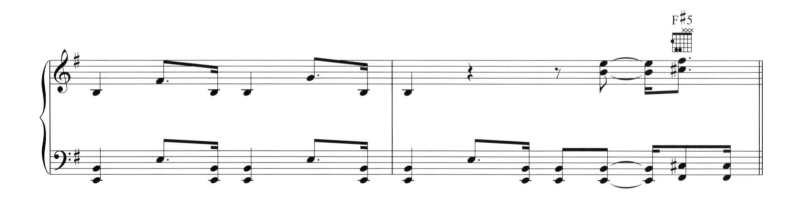

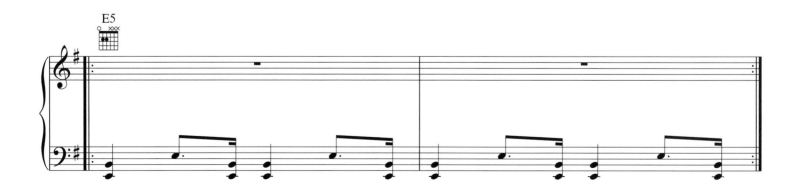

Play 3 times

Yeah,   you can't front on that.

Play 5 times

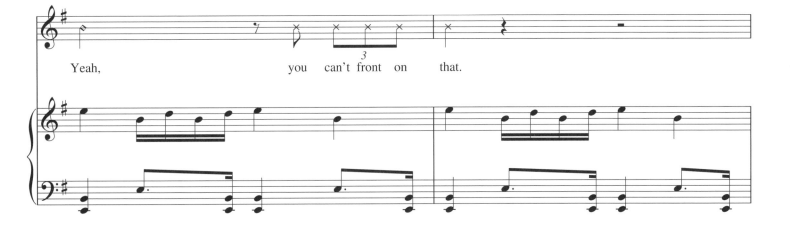

Yeah,   you can't front on   that.

Em11

Play 3 times

So

what-'cha, what - 'cha, what -'cha want?What -'cha want? So what-'cha, what - 'cha, what-'cha want? So what-'cha want? I said,

what-'cha, what - 'cha, what-'cha want? What -'cha want? I said, what-'cha, what - 'cha, what-'cha want?Said, what-'cha want?

Rap Lyrics

Rap 1: Well, just plug me in just like I was Eddie Harris. You're eatin' crazy cheeze like you would think I'm from Paris.
You know I get fly. You think I get high. You know that I'm gone and I'm gon' tell you all why.
So tell me, who are you dissin'? Maybe I'm missin' the reason that you're smilin' and wildin'.
So listen in my head, I just wanna take 'em down. Imagination set loose and I'm gonna shake 'em down.
Let it flow like a mud slide, and when I get on I like to ride and glide.
I got depth of perception in my text, y'all. I get props at my mention 'cause I vex y'all.

Rap 2: Well, they call me Mike D. the ever lovin' man. I'm like Spoonie Gee. Well, I'm the metropolitician.
You scream and you holla 'bout my Chevy Impala but the sweat is gettin' wet around the ring around your collar.
But like a dream I'm flowin' without no stoppin'. Sweeter than a cherry pie with Ready-Whip toppin'.
But mic to mic, kickin' the wall to wall. Well, I'll be callin' out to people like a castin' call.
A-well it's whack when you're jacked in the back of my ride with your know, with your flow when you're out gettin' by.
Believe me, a-what you see is what you get, and you see me, I'm comin' off as you can bet.
Well, I think I'm losin' my mind this time. This time I'm losin' my mind.
That's right, said I think I'm losin' my mind this time. This time I'm losin' my mind.

Rap 3: But little do you know about somethin' that I talk about. I'm tired of drivin', it's due time that I walk about.
But in the meantime I'm wise to the demise. Got eyes in the back of my head so I realize.
A-well I'm Dr. Spock, I'm here to rock y'all. I want you off the wall if you're playin' the wall.
I said, what'cha, what'cha, what'cha want? Well, what'cha want? I said, what'cha, what'cha, what'cha want?
A-what'cha want? Y'all suckers write me checks and then they bounce, so I reach into my pocket for the fresh amount.
See, I'm a long leaner. This is the cleaner. I'm the illest motherfucker from here to Gardena.
Well, I'm as cool as a cucumber in a bowl of hot sauce, so once you get my rhyme and reason but got no cause.
Well, if you're hot to trot, you think you're slicker than grease.
I got news for your crews, you'll be suckin' like a leech.

BRASS MONKEY

Words and Music by MICHAEL DIAMOND,
ADAM HOROVITZ, ADAM YAUCH
and RICK RUBIN

Moderate Rap

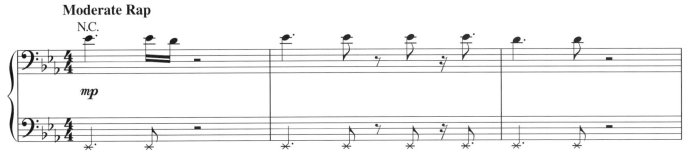

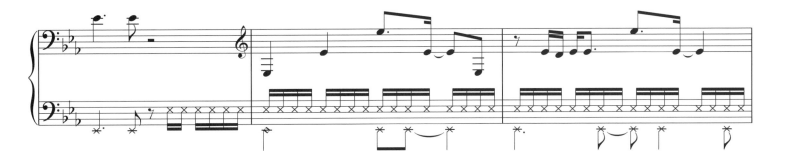

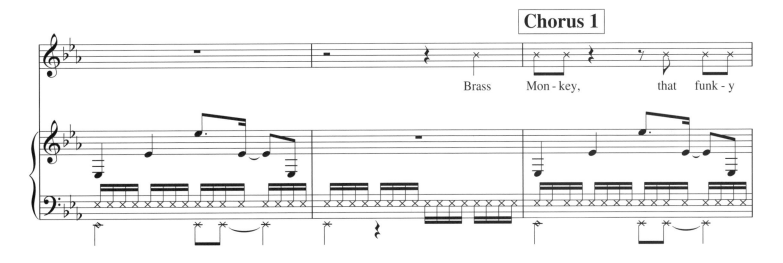

Chorus 1

Brass Mon-key, that funk-y mon-key.

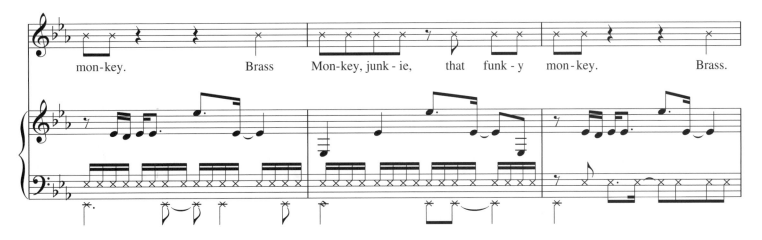

mon-key. Brass Mon-key, junk-ie, that funk-y mon-key. Brass.

Rap 1

Play 3 times

Chorus 2

Brass Mon-key, that funk-y mon-key. Brass Mon-key, junk-ie, that funk-y mon-key. Brass.

Rap 3

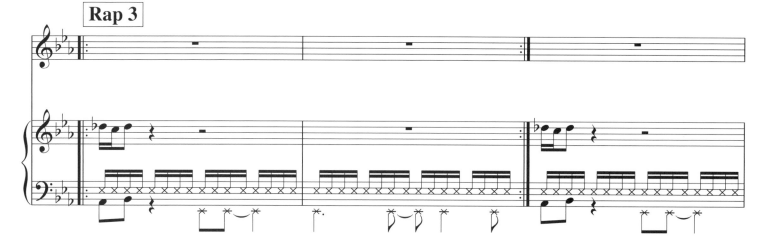

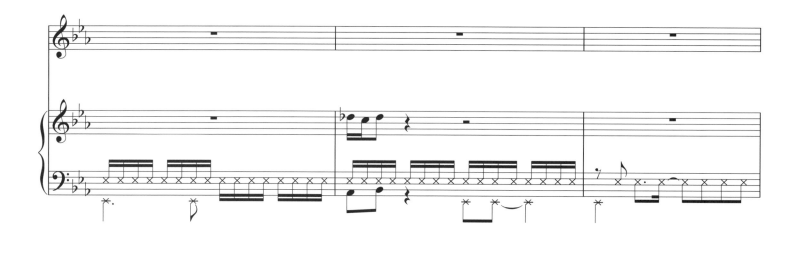

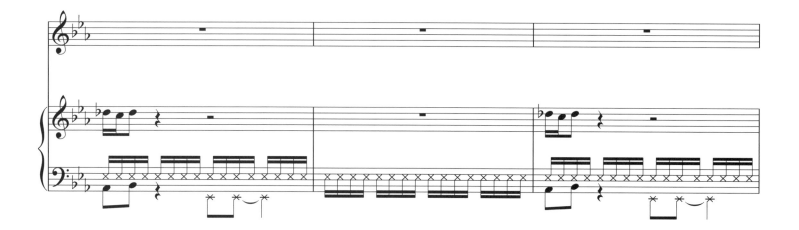

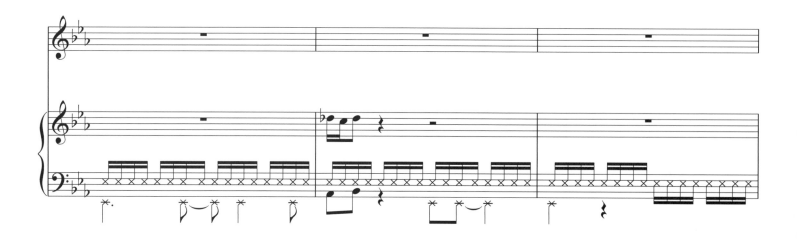

Chorus 4

Brass Mon - key, that funk - y

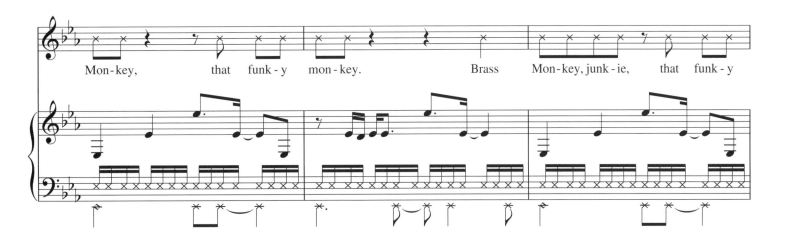

mon - key. Brass Mon - key, junk - ie, that funk - y mon - key. Brass.

Mon - key, that funk - y mon - key. Brass Mon - key, junk - ie, that funk - y

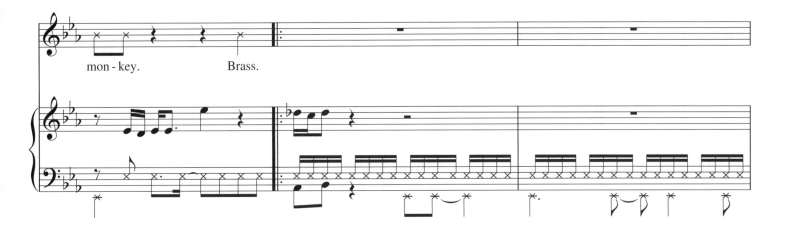

mon - key. Brass.

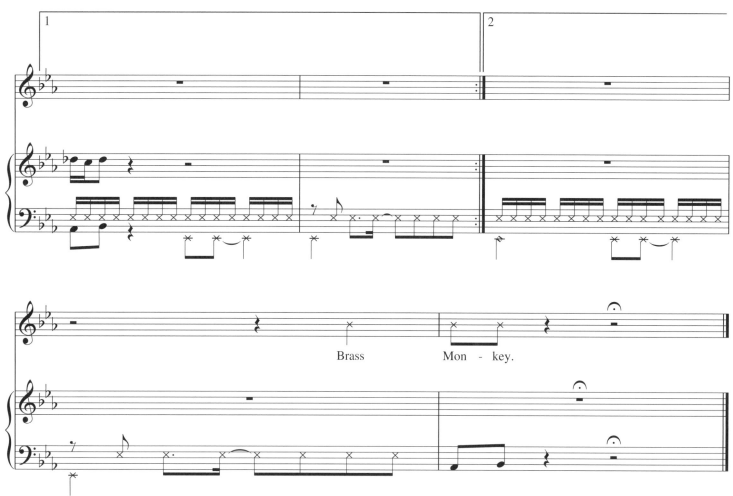

Additional Lyrics

Chorus 1: Brass Monkey, that funky monkey. Brass Monkey, junkie, that funky monkey. Brass.

Rap 1: Got this dance that's more than real, drink Brass Monkey here's how you feel.
You put your left leg down, your right leg up. Tilt your head back, let's finish the cup.
M.C.A. with the bottle, D. rocks the can. Adrock get's nice with Charlie Chan.
We're offered Moet, we don't mind Chivas. Wherever we go we bring the Monkey with us.
Adrock drinks three, Mike D. is D. Double R. foots the bill most definately.
I drink Brass Monkey and I rock well. Got a castle in Brooklyn, that's where I dwell.

Chorus 2: Brass Monkey, that funky monkey. Brass Monkey, junkie, that funky monkey. Brass.

Rap 2: I drink it anytime and anyplace. When it's time to get ill, I pour it on my face.
Monkey tastes def when you pour it on ice, come on y'all it's time to get nice.
Coolin' by the lockers, gettin' kinda' funky. Me and the crew, we're drinkin' Brass Monkey.
This girl walked by, she gave me the eye. I reached in the locker, grabbed the Spanish Fly.
I put it in the Monkey and mixed it in a cup, went over to the girl, "Yo baby, wassup?"
I offered her a sip, sip. The girl, she gave me lip. lip.
It did begin, the stuff wore in and now she's on my....

Chorus 3: Brass Monkey, that funky monkey. Brass Monkey, junkie, that funky monkey. Brass.

Rap 3: Step up to the bar and put the girl down. She takes a big gulp and slaps it around.
You take a sip if you can do it, you get right to it. We had a case in the place, well we went right through it.
You got a dry Martini, you're thinkin' you're cool. Take your place at the bar, smack you off your stool.
I'll down a forty dog in a single gulp and if you got beef, you get beat to a pulp.
Monkey and parties and reelin' and rockin'. Def, def, girls, girls, all y'all jockin'.
The song and dance keepin' you in a trance. If you don't buy my record, I got my advance.
I drink it, I think it. I see it, I be it. I love Brass Monkey but I won't give D. it.
We got the bottle, you got the cup. Come on everybody let's get fffffff.

Chorus 4: Brass Monkey, that funky monkey. Brass Monkey, junkie, that funky monkey. (Repeat)

CH-CHECK IT OUT

Words and Music by MICHAEL DIAMOND,
ADAM HOROVITZ and ADAM YAUCH

Moderate Rap

Rap 1: *(See Rap lyrics)*

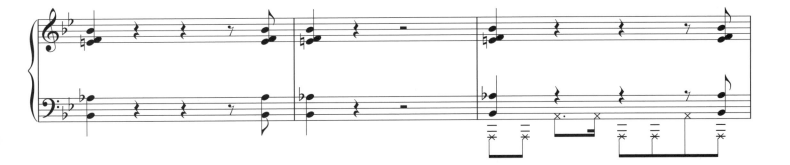

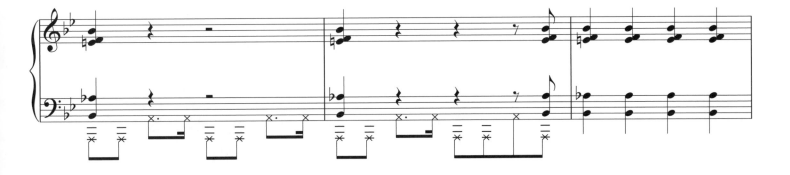

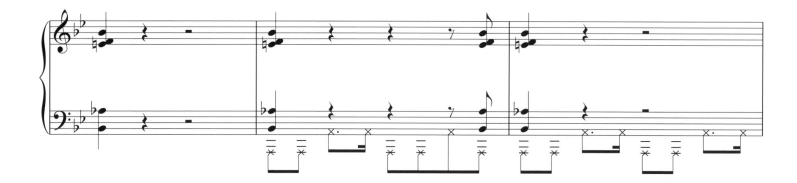

Bb7b5

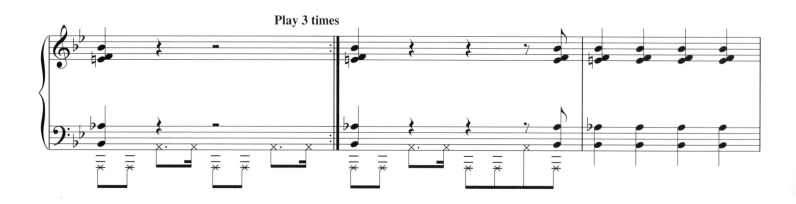

Play 3 times

REFRAIN 1

Check, ch - check, check, check, __ ch - check it out.   What, wha - what, what, what's it all about.

Work, wa - work, work, work, wa - work it out. Let's turn this motherfuckin' party out. __

Bb7b5

Play 3 times

Rap 2
Rap 3

Bb7b5

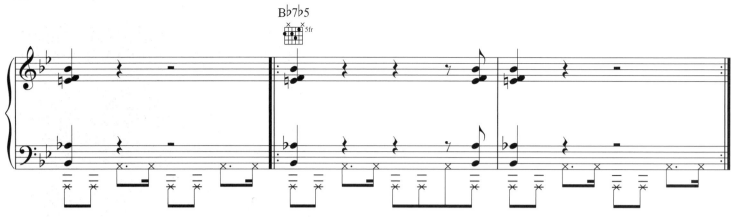

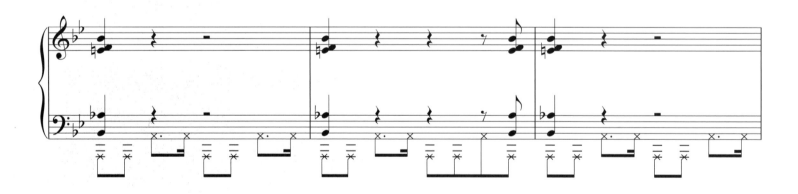

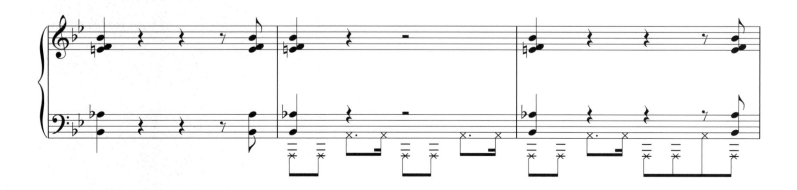

REFRAIN 2
REFRAIN 3

Check, ch - check, check, check, ch - check it out.

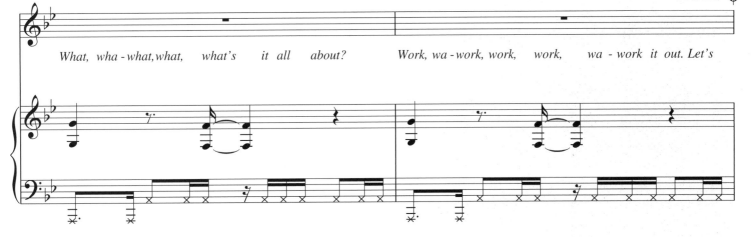

What, wha - what, what, what's it all about? Work, wa - work, work, work, wa - work it out. Let's

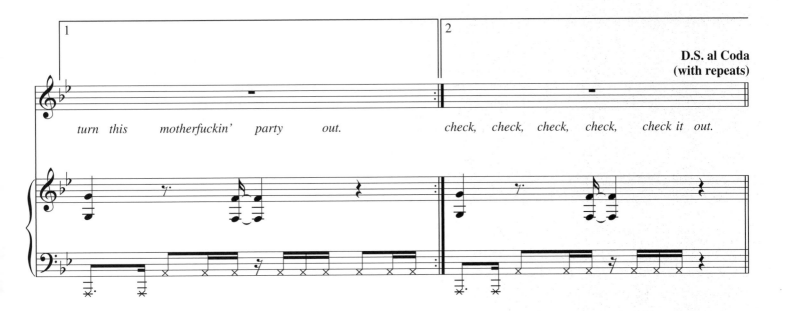

turn this motherfuckin' party out.   *check, check, check, check, check it out.*

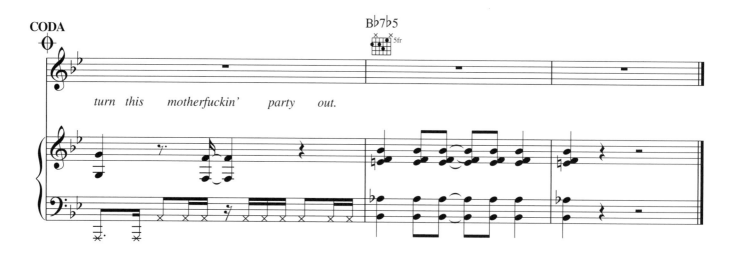

turn this motherfuckin' party out.

Rap Lyrics

Rap 1: All you Trekkies and TV addicts, don't mean to dis, don't mean to bring static.
All you Klingons in the fuckin' house, grab your backstreet friend and get loud. Blowin' doors off hinges.
Grab you with the pinchers. And no, I didn't retire. I'll snatch you up with the needle nose pliers.
Like Mutual of Omaha with the ill boat you never seen before. Glidin' in the glades and like Lorne Greene, you know
I get paid. Like caprese with the basil. Not goofy like Darren or Hazel. I'm a motherfuckin' Nick at Night with
Classics rerunnin' that you know all right. Now remain calm, no alarm 'cause my farm ain't fat. So what's up with that?
I got friends and family that I respect. When I think I'm too good, they put me in check. So believe when I say I'm no
Better than you, except when I rap, so I guess it ain't true. Like that y'all and you just don't stop, guaranteed to make
Your body rock.

Refrain 1: Check, ch-check, check, check, ch-check it out. What, wha-what, what, what's it all about?
Work, wa-work, work, work, wa-work it out. Let's turn this motherfuckin' party out.

Rap 2: Said, "Doc, what's the condition? I'm a man that's on a mission." He said, "Son, you'd better listen, stuck in your
Ass is an electrician." Like a scientist, mm, when I'm applyin' this method of controllin' my mind like Einstein
And Rappin' Duke combined. Now, hey baby, bubba now, what's the deal? I didn't know you go for that mass appeal.
Some call it salugi, some hot potato. I stole your mic but you won't see it later 'cause I work magic like a magician.
I add up the mathematician. I'm a bank cashier, engineer. I wear cotton and I don't wear sheer. Shazam and abracadabra.
In the whip, I'm gonna cruise past you. Yo money, don't chump yourself. Put that shit back on the shelf.
Light rays blazin', you're out of phase and my crew's amazin'. We're workin' on the record yo so just stay patient.

Refrain 2: Check, ch-check, check, check, ch-check it out. What, wha-what, what, what's it all about?
Work, wa-work, work, work, wa-work it out. Let's turn this motherfuckin' party out.
Check, ch-check, check, check, ch-check it out. What, wha-what, what, what's it all about?
Work, wa-work, work, work, wa-work it out.
Let's check, check, check, check, check it out.

Rap 3: Now, I go by the name of The King Adrock. I don't wear a cup nor a jock. I bring the shit that's beyond bizarre.
Like Miss Piggy, "Who, Moi?" I am the one with the clientele. You say, "Adrock, you rock so well."
I got class like Pink Champale. M.C.A., grab the mic before the mic goes stale. Don't test me. They can't arrest me.
I'll fake right, crossover and shoot lefty. You look upset yo, calm down. You look like Cable Guy dunked off of
Your crown. I flow like smoke out of a chimney. You never been me. You wanna rap but your record ain't hip hop B.
Now, get your clothes right out the dryer. Put Armor All up on the tire. Sport that fresh attire. Tonight we're goin'
Out, set the town on fire. Set the town ablaze. Gonna stun and amaze. Ready to throw a craze.
Make your granny shake her head and say, "Those were the days."

Refrain 3: Now, check, ch-check, check, check, ch-check it out. What, wha-what, what, what's it all about?
Work, wa-work, work, work, wa-work it out. Let's turn this motherfuckin' party out.

NO SLEEP 'TIL BROOKLYN

Words and Music by RICK RUBIN,
ADAM HOROVITZ, ADAM YAUCH
and MICHAEL DIAMOND

Moderate Rap Rock

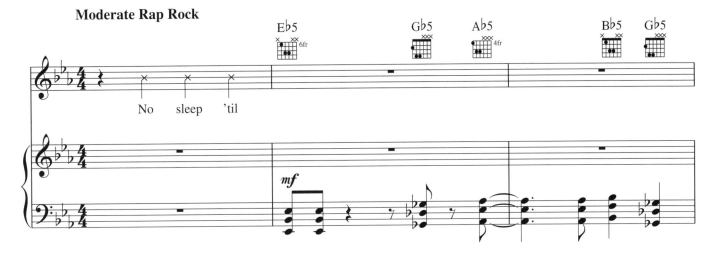

No sleep 'til

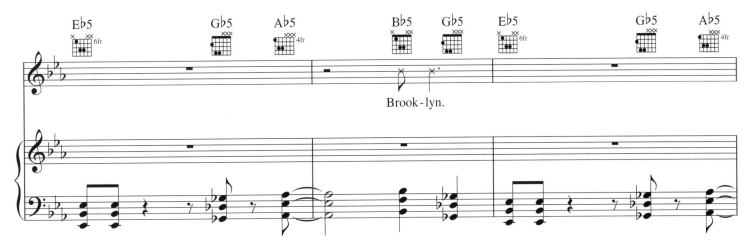

Brook-lyn.

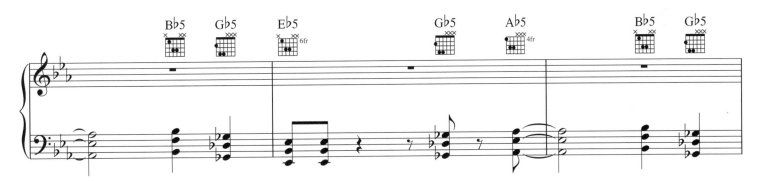

Rap 1

Chorus 1

No sleep 'til....

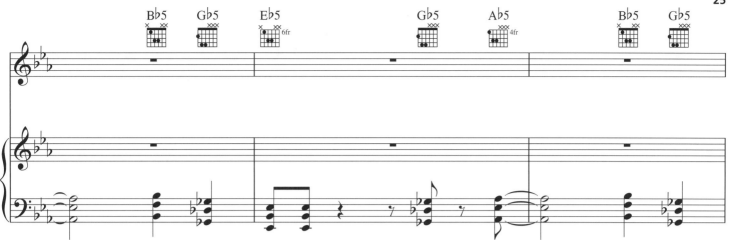

Rap 2

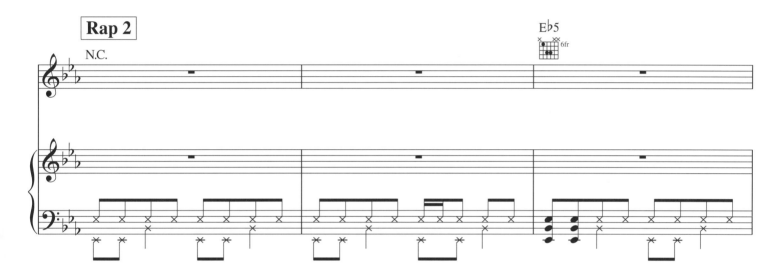

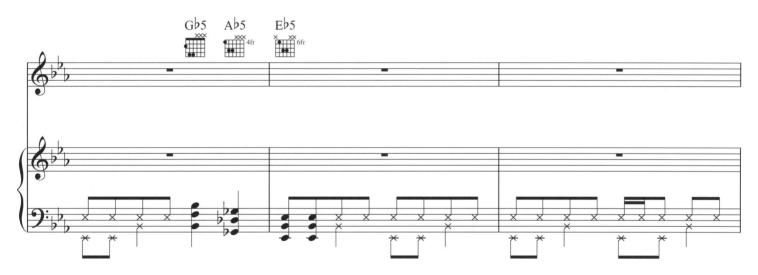

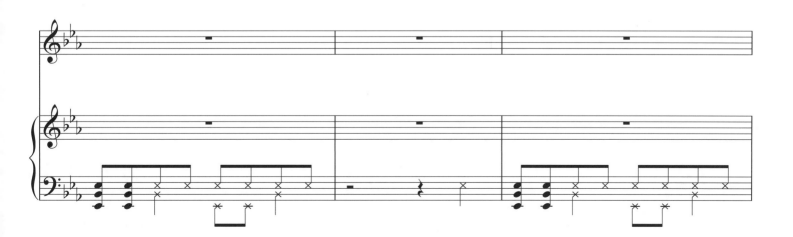

Chorus 2

Rap 3

Chorus 3

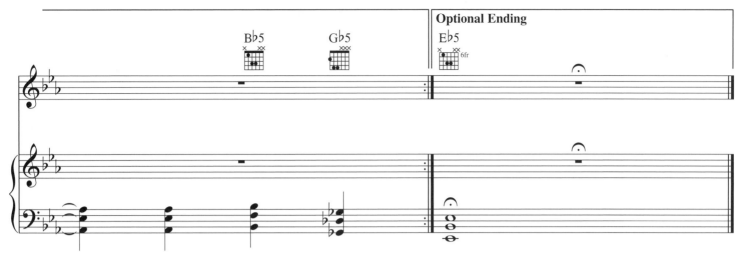

Additional Lyrics

Rap 1: Foot on the pedal, never ever force metal. Engine runnin' hotter than a boiling kettle.
My job ain't a job, it's a damn good time. City to city I'm runnin' my rhymes.
On location, tourin' 'round the nation. Beastie Boys always on vacation.
Itchy trigger finger but a stable turntable. I do what I do best because I'm illin' and able.
Ain't no fakin', your money I'm takin'. Goin' coast to coast and watch all the girlies shakin'.
While you're at the job workin' nine to five, the Beastie Boys at the Garden cold kickin' it live.

Chorus 1: No sleep 'til....
Another plane, another train, another bottle in the brain.
Another girl, another fight, another drive all night.

Rap 2: Our manager's crazy, he always smokes dust. He's got his own room at the back of the bus.
Tour around the world, you rock around the clock. Plane to hotel, girls on the jock.
Trashin' hotels like it's goin' out of style. Gettin' paid along the way 'cause it's worth your while.
Four on the floor, Adrock's out the door. M.C.A.'s in the back 'cause he's skeezin' with a whore.
We got a safe in the trunk with money in a stack, with dice in the front and Brooklyn's in the back.

Chorus 2: No sleep 'til.
No sleep 'til Brooklyn.
No sleep 'til Brooklyn.
Ain't seen the light since we started this band, M.C.A., get on the mic my man.

Rap 3: Born and bred in Brooklyn, the U.S.A. They call me Adam Yauch, but I'm the M.C.A.
Like a lemon to a lime, a lime to a lemon, I sip a def ale with all the fine women.
Limos, arenas and TV shows. Autographed pictures and classy hos.
Step off homes, get out of my way. Tax little girlies from here to LA.
Wakin' up before I get to sleep 'cause I'll be rockin' this party eight days a week.

Chorus 3: No sleep 'til....
No sleep 'til Brooklyn.
No sleep 'til Brooklyn.
No, (no,) sleep, (sleep,) 'til Brooklyn, (Brooklyn.)
No, (no,) sleep, (sleep,) 'til Brooklyn, yeah.

Chorus 4: No, (no,) sleep, (sleep,) 'til Brooklyn, (Brooklyn.) *(Repeat as needed.)*

HEY LADIES

Words and Music by BARBARELLA BISHOP,
MICHAEL DIAMOND, MATT DIKE, RONALD FORD,
ADAM HOROVITZ, JOHN KING, GARRY SHIDER,
LINDA SHIDER, MICHAEL SIMPSON, LARRY TROUTMAN,
ROGER TROUTMAN and ADAM YAUCH

Rap 1: *(See Rap lyrics)*

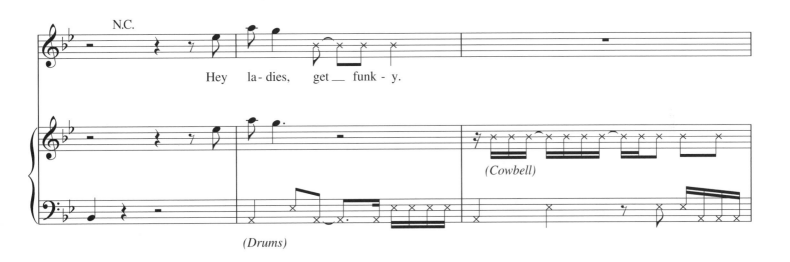

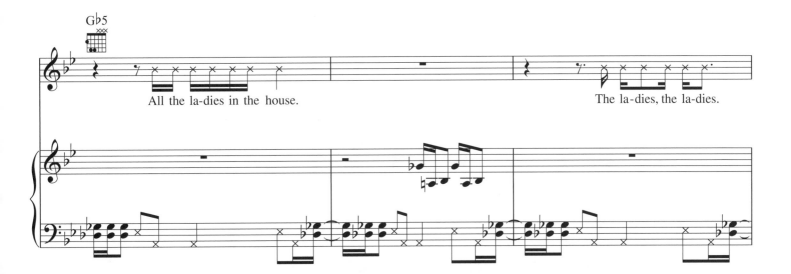

Rap 2

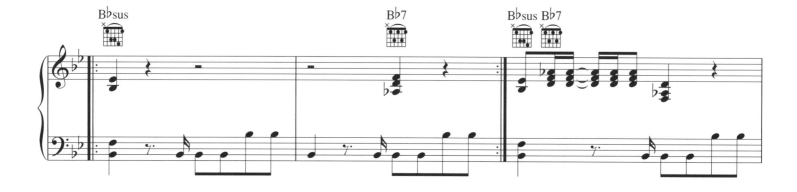

(Drums)

in it, funk - y. You know that... **Rap 3**

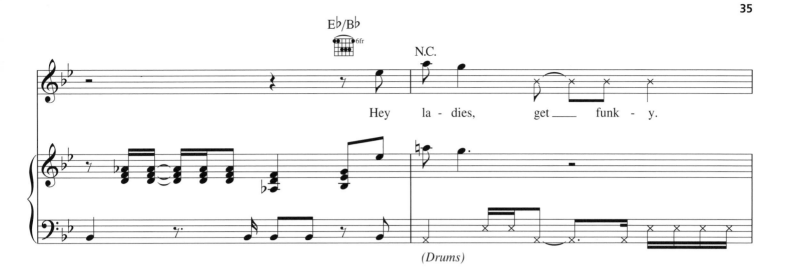

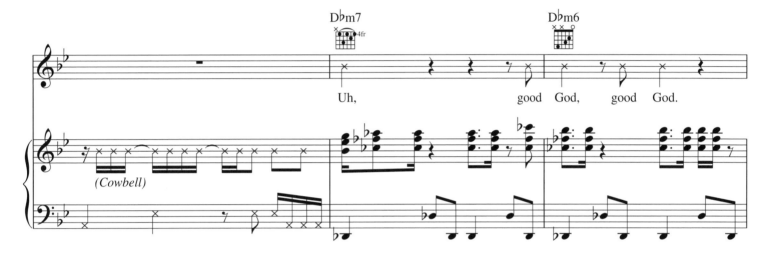

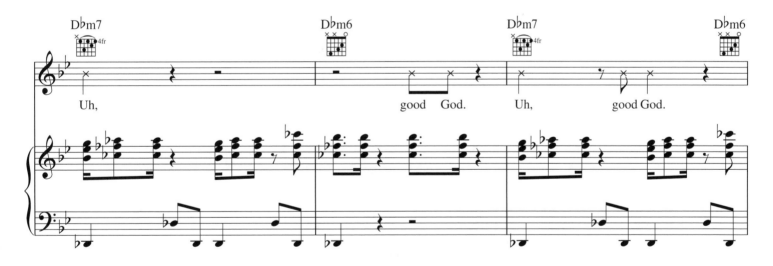

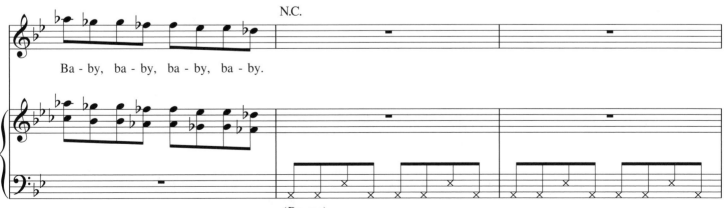

Rap Lyrics

Rap 1: Hey ladies in the place, I'm callin' out to y'all. There never was a city kid truer and bluer.
There's more to me than you'll ever know and I got more hits than Sadaharu Oh.
Tom Thumb, Tom Cushman or tom foolery. I date women on TV with the help of Chuck Woolery.
Words are flowin' out just like the Grand Canyon, and I'm always out lookin' for a female companion.
I threw the lasso 'round the tallest one and dragged her to the crib. I took off her moccasins and put on my bib.
Wheelin' and dealin', I make a little bit of a stealin'. I'll bring you back to the place and your dress I'm peelin'.
Your body's on time and your mind is appealin'. Starin' at the cracks up there upon the ceilin'.
Such and such will be the place that I'm doin'. I'm talkin' to the girl tellin' her I'm all-knowin'.
She's talkin' to the kid. Who? Talkin' to the kid. I'm tellin' her every lie that you know that I never did.

Rap 2: Well, me in the corner with a good-lookin' daughter. I dropped my drawers, she said, "Welcome back, Kotter."
We was cuttin' up the rug, she started cuttin' up the carpet. In my apartment I beg her, "Please stop it."
Well, the gift of gab is the gift that I have and then that girl ain't nothin' but a crab. Educated no, stupid yep,
And when I say stupid I mean stupid fresh. I'm not James at fifteen or Chachi in charge.
I'm Adam and I'm adamant about livin' large, oh, with the white Sassoons and then the looks that kill.
Makin' love in the back of my Coupe de Ville. I met a little cutie, she was all hopped up on zootie.
I liked the little cutie but I kicked her in the bootie 'cause I don't gotta go for that messin' around.
You been listenin' to my records, A number one sound. Just step to the rhythm. Step, step to the ride.
I've got an open mind so why don't you all get inside? Tune in, turn on to a tune that's live.
Ladies flock like bees to a hive.

Rap 3: She got a gold tooth. You know she's hard-core. She'll show you a good time, then she'll show you the door.
Break up with your girl, it ended in tears. Vincent Van Gogh gon' mail that ear.
I call her in the middle of the night when I'm drinkin'. The phone booth on the corner is damp and it's stinkin'.
She said come on over, it was me that she missed. I threw the trash can through her window 'cause you know I got dissed.
Your old lady left you and you went insane. You blew yourself up in the back of the six train.
Take my advice at any price. A gorilla like your mother is mighty weak.
Suckin' down pints until I didn't know. Woke up in the mornin' with the one ton ho.
'Cause I announce I like girls that bounce, with the weight that pays about a pound per ounce.
Girls with curls and big, long locks and beatnik chicks just wearin' their smocks.
Walkin' high and mighty like she's number one. She thinks she's the passionate one.

PASS THE MIC

Words and Music by MICHAEL DIAMOND,
ADAM HOROVITZ, ADAM YAUCH
and MARIO CALDATO JR.

Moderate Rap

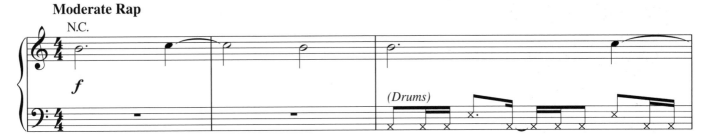

Rap 1: *(See Rap lyrics)*

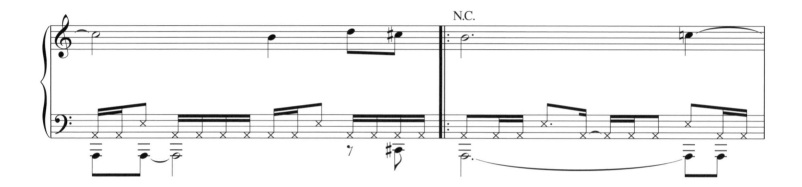

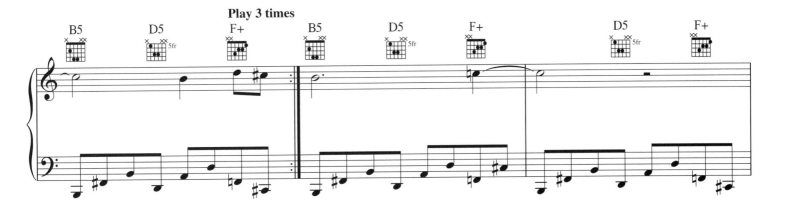

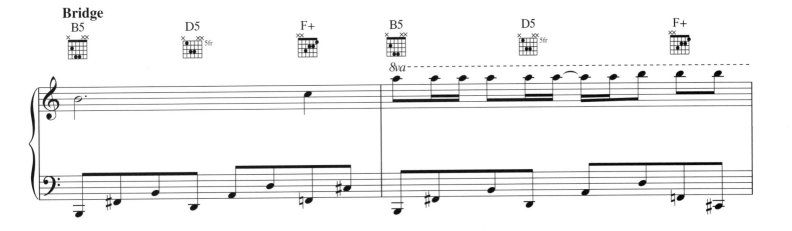

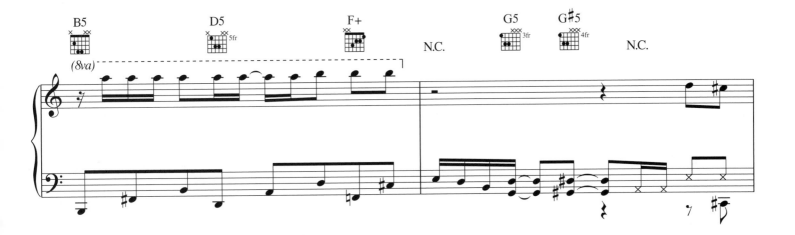

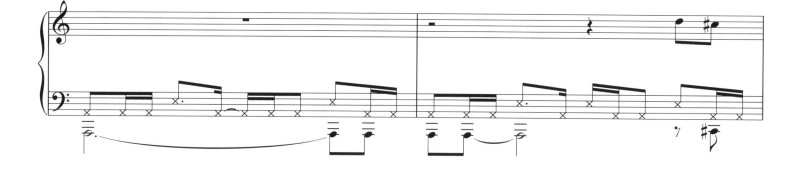

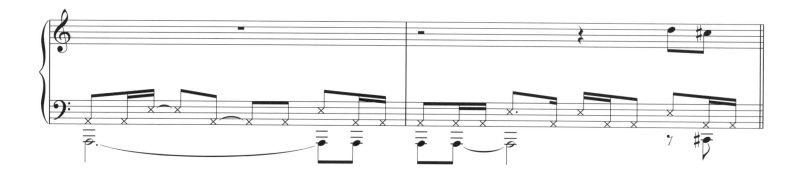

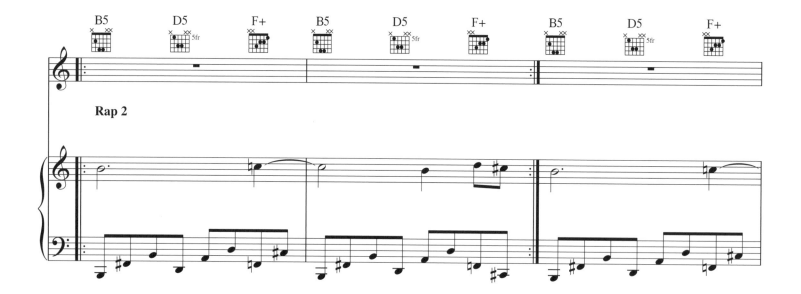

Rap 2

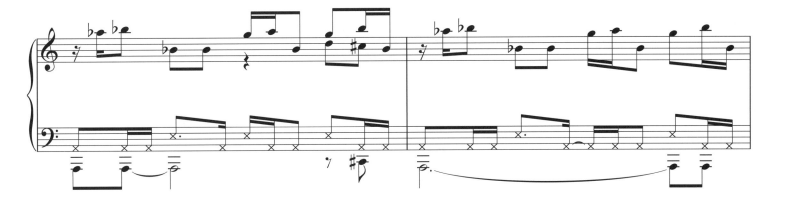

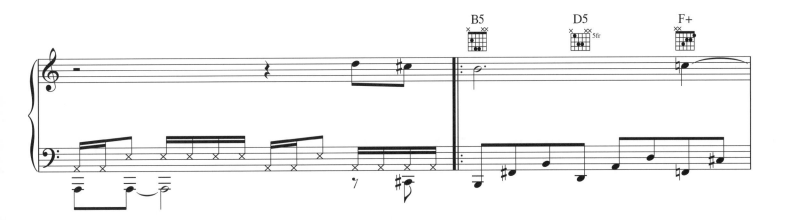

Play 4 times

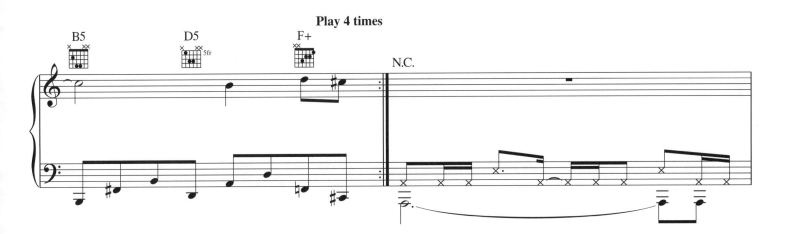

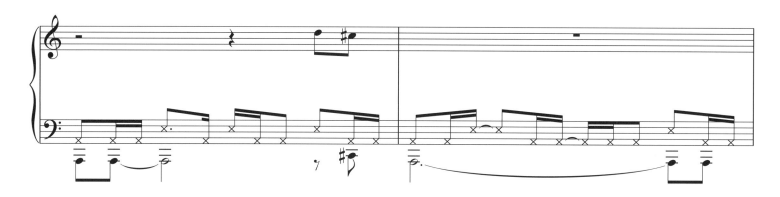

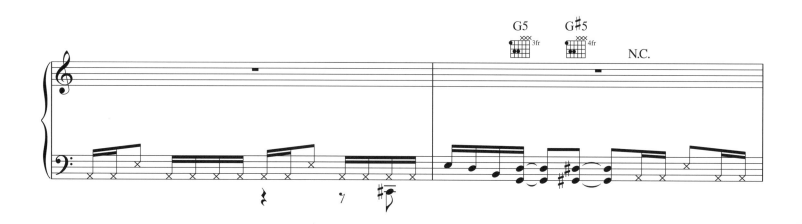

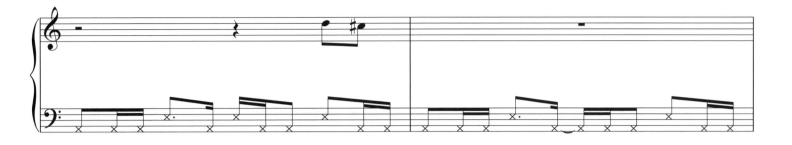

Rap ends

Rap Lyrics

Rap 1: If you can do what I'm doin', then it's a musical masterpiece. Hear what I'm dealin' with and that's cool, at least.
What's runnin' through my mind comes through in my walk. True feelings are shown from the way that I talk.
And this is me, y'all. I M.C. y'all. My name is M.C.A. and I still do what I please.
And now I'd like to introduce, what's up, I'll pass the mic to D. for a fistful of truth. The name is D. y'all, and I don't play,
And I can rock a block party 'til your hair turns grey. So what you sayin'? I explode on site and like Jimmy Walker,
"I'm dynomite." And now I'd like to pass the mic so Adrock c'mon and do anything you like. I'm the A.D.R.O.C.K.
In the place with the bass I'm goin' all the way. I can't stop, y'all, tock, tick, y'all.
And if you think that you're slick, you'll catch a brick, y'all, 'cause I'm a turn it in and I'm a turn it out.
But now I gotta pass the mike to Yauch. Yeah, on and on and on and on. I can't stop, y'all, until the early morn.
So rock, rock, y'all. A tick tock, y'all a-to the beat, y'all. A-c'mon and rock, y'all. I give thanks for inspiration.
It guides my mind along the way. A lotta people get jealous. They're talkin' about me but that's just 'cause they
Haven't got a thing to say.

Rap 2: C'mon everybody rappin' like it's a commercial. Acting like life is a big commercial. So this is what I got to say to you all.
Be true to yourself and you will never fall. And now I'd like to pass the mic to the A. So what's your name, Yauch?
My name is M.C.A. I been comin' to where I am from the get go. Find that I can groove with the beat when I let go.
So put your worries on hold, get up and groove with the rhythm in your soul.
And now I'd like to pass the mic to my brother Adrock. C'mon and shine like a light. Yes, yes, y'all, and yes, yes, y'all.
I'm always on time, nevertheless, y'all. And that's right, y'all, I shed light, y'all. I got no time in my life to get uptight, y'all.
So what'cha gonna say that I don't know already? I'm like Clyde and I'm rockin' steady.
But time flies when you're havin' fun, so Mike D., that's me, c'mon and get some. M.I.K.E. to the D.
You come to see me and you pay a fee. Do what I do professionally. To tell the truth, I am exactly what I want to be.
Now Adrock and M.C.A. let's rock this joint in the old school way. Well, rock on 'til the crack of dawn.
Mowin' down M.C.'s like I'm mowin' a lawn. I go off like nothin' can phase me. You think we'll ever meet Stevie?
One of these days, D. But I can stand my ground and I am down to watch an M.C. who acts like a clown.
But for now, I'd like to ask you how you like the feel of the bass in your face in the crowd.

AN OPEN LETTER TO NYC

Words and Music by MICHAEL DIAMOND,
ADAM HOROVITZ, ADAM YAUCH,
EUGENE O'CONNOR and DAVID THOMAS

Lis-ten, all you New York-ers. ___

Moderate Hip-Hop

Chorus 1

Rap 1

Play 4 times **Chorus 2**

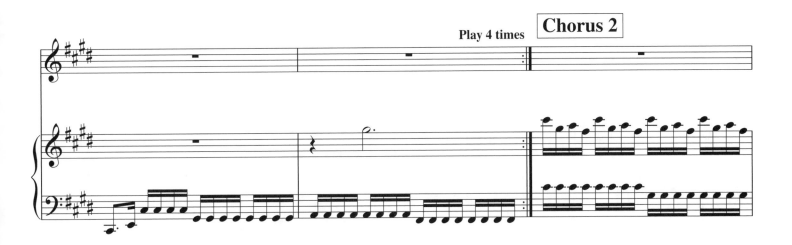

Rap 2

Play 4 times **Chorus 3**

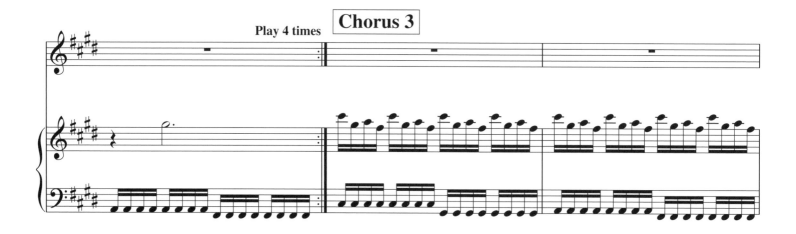

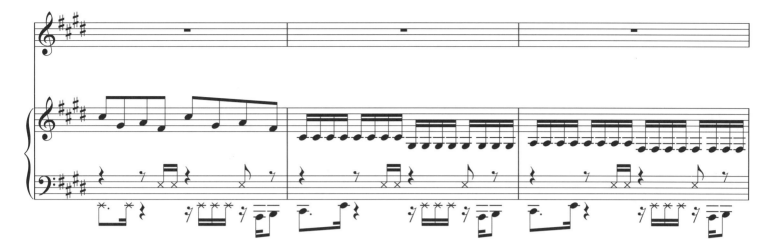

Rap 3

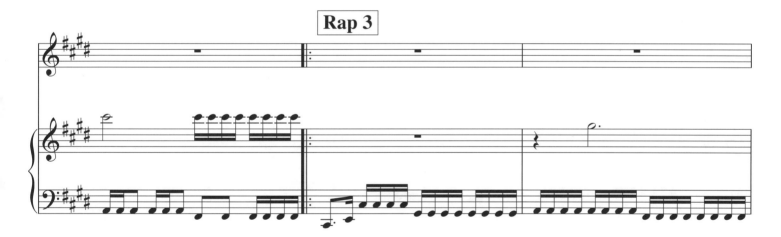

Play 4 times

Chorus 4

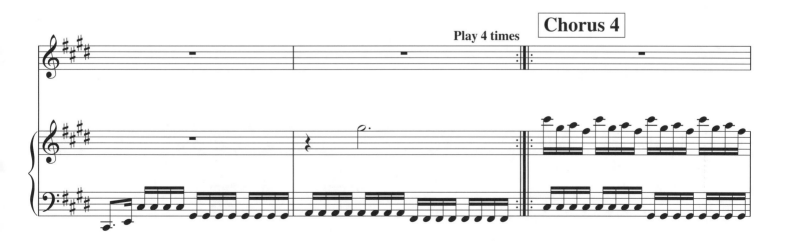

New, New, New, New York.

New York, New York Cit-y, Cit-y. New, New York, New,

New, New, New York, New York Cit-y. Hey, hey, hey,hey, hey, hey New York, New

Additional Lyrics

Chorus 1: Brooklyn, Bronx, Queens and Staten. Brooklyn Battery to the top of Manhattan.
Asian, Middle Eastern and Latin, Black, White, New York, you make it happen.

Rap 1: Brownstones, water towers, trees, skyscrapers, writers, prize fighters and Wall Street traders.
We come together on the subway cars. Diversity unified, whoever you are.
Uhh, we doin' fine on the One and Nine line. On the L, we doin' swell. On the number Ten bus, we fight and fuss.
You know we're thorough in the boroughs 'cause that's a must. I remember when the Deuce was all porno flicks.
Runnin' home after school to play PIX. At lunch I'd go to Blimpies down on Montague Street and hit the
Fulton Street Mall for the sneakers on my feet. Dear New York, I hope you're doin' well.
I know a lot's happened and you been through hell. So, we give thanks for providin' a home.
Through your gates at Ellis Island we passed in droves.

Chorus 2: Brooklyn, Bronx, Queens and Staten. Brooklyn Battery to the top of Manhattan.
Asian, Middle Eastern and Latin, Black, White, New York, you make it happen.

Rap 2: The L.I.E., the B.Q.E. Hippies at the band shell with the L.S.D. Get my BVD's from VIM.
You know I'm reppin' Manhattan the best I can. Stopped off at Bleeker Bob's, got thrown out.
Sneakin' in at 4AM after goin' out. You didn't rob me in the park at Diana Ross but everybody started
Lootin' when the lights went off. From the south, South Bronx on out to Queens Bridge.
From Hollis Queens right down to Bay Ridge. From Castle Hill to the Lower East Side.
From 1010 WINS to Live At Five. Dear New York, this is a love letter to you and how you brought us together.
We can't say enough about all you do 'cause in the city we're ourselves and electric, too.

Chorus 3: Brooklyn, Bronx, Queens and Staten. Brooklyn Battery to the top of Manhattan.
sian, Middle Eastern and Latin, Black, White, New York, you make it happen.

Rap 3: Shout out the South Bronx where my mom hails from. Right next to High Bridge, across from Harlem.
To the Grand Concourse where my mom and dad met before they moved on down to the Upper West.
I see you're still strong after all that's goin' on. Life long, we dedicate this song.
Just a little somethin' to show some respect to the city that blends and mends and tests.
Uhh, since 9/11 we're still livin' and lovin' life we been given. Ain't nothin' gonna take it away from us.
We're lookin' pretty and gritty 'cause in the city we trust. Dear New York, I know a lot has changed.
Two towers down but you're still in the game. Home to the many, rejecting no one.
Acceptin' peoples of all places wherever they're from.

Chorus 4: Brooklyn, Bronx, Queens and Staten. Brooklyn Battery to the top of Manhattan.
Asian, Middle Eastern and Latin, Black, White, New York, you make it happen. *(Repeat)*

ROOT DOWN

Words and Music by MICHAEL DIAMOND,
ADAM YAUCH and ADAM HOROVITZ

Moderate Funky Rap

down-town Brook-lyn is where I was born but when the snow is fall - in', then I am gone. And

you might think that I'm a fa-nat-ic. A phone call from U - tah and I'm throw-in' a pan - ic. So

break it to the root, where we kick it on down. Jim-my Smith is my man, I wan-na give him a pound. I kick it

root down. I put my root down. I kick it root down. I put my root down. So

how you wan-na kick it? Gon-na kick it root down. So how we gon-na kick it? Gon-na kick it root down. So

how we gon-na kick it? Gon-na kick it root down. Break it on down, gon-na kick it root down.

Bbm6   G(add9)/B   Cm7   C#m7b5   Dm11   Bbm6   G(add9)/B   Cm7

C#m7b5   Dm11   N.C.

I'm Ad - rock, huh?____ I don't stop, come on.____ I just

nough of that, just wan-na give __ some re-spect __ due M. C. A. Grab the mic and Ma Bell __ will con-nect __ you. Bob

Mar - ley was a proph - et for the free - dom fight. ___ Give thanks and

praise to the Lord and I will feel al - right. __ I feel I'm good to play a lit-tle mu - sic, ___ tears are

run - nin' down my face 'cause I love to do it. And no one ___ can stop this flow from flow-in' on. __ A flow mas-

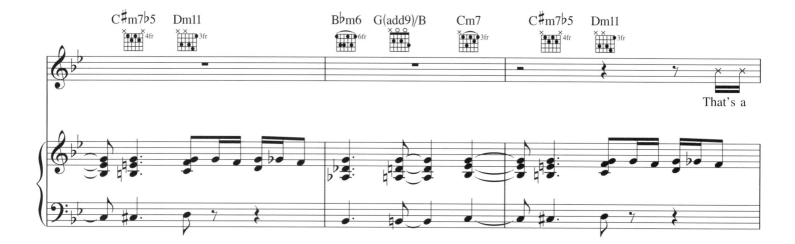

SHAKE YOUR RUMP

Words and Music by MICHAEL DIAMOND,
ADAM HOROVITZ, ADAM YAUCH, JOHN KING,
MICHAEL SIMPSON and MATT DIKE

Moderate funky Rap

Rap 1

Recorded a half step higher.

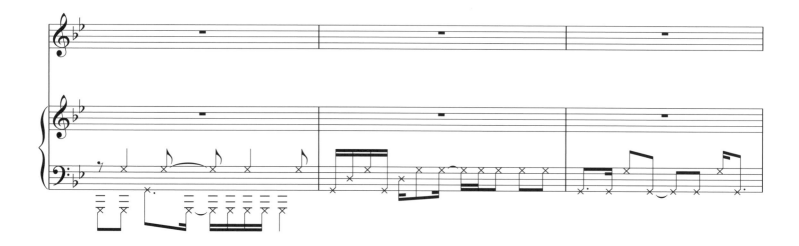

It's the joint.

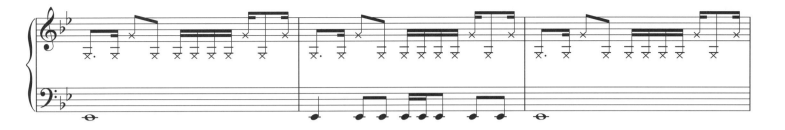

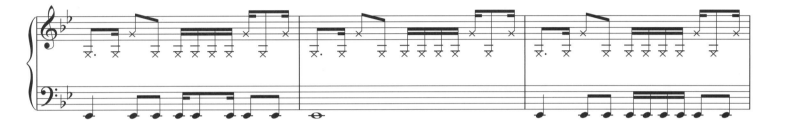

Rap 2

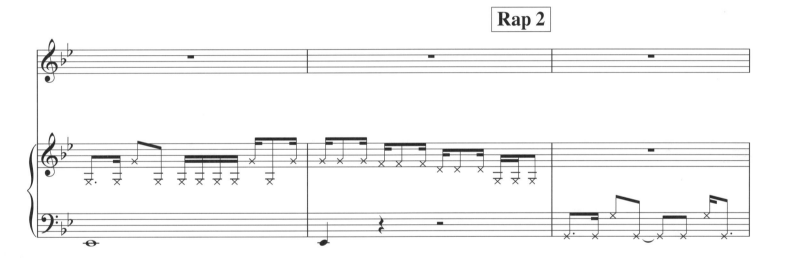

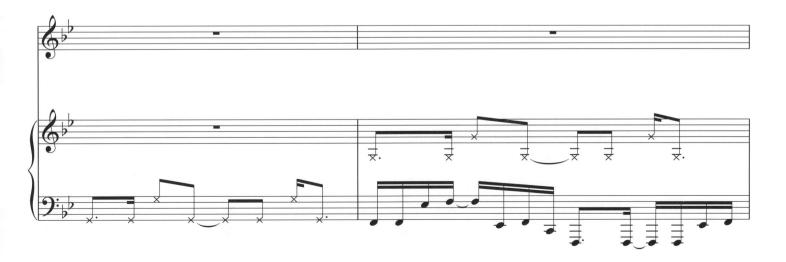

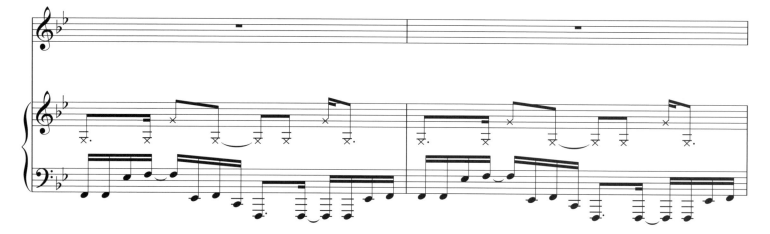

D♭m

N.C.

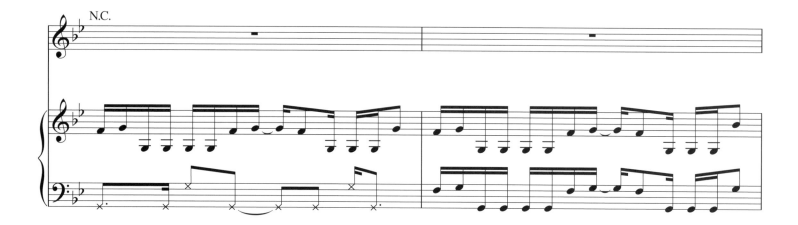

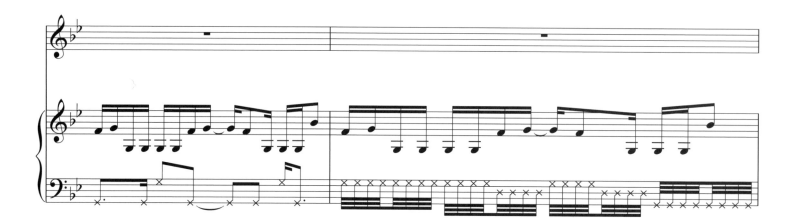

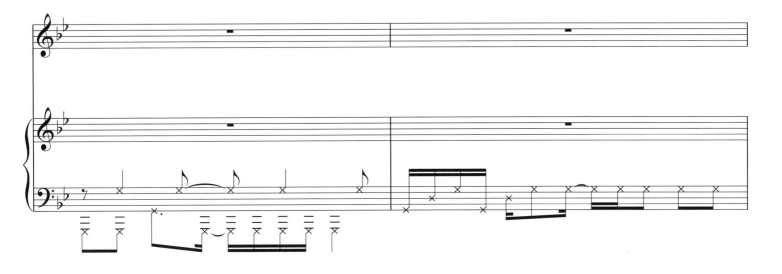

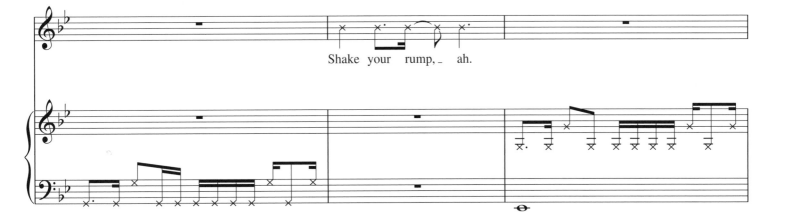

Shake your rump,_ ah.

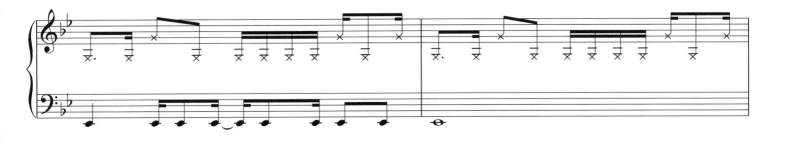

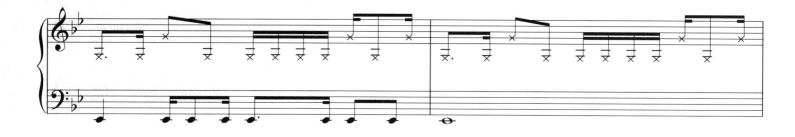

Rap 3

(Bubbling water sound)

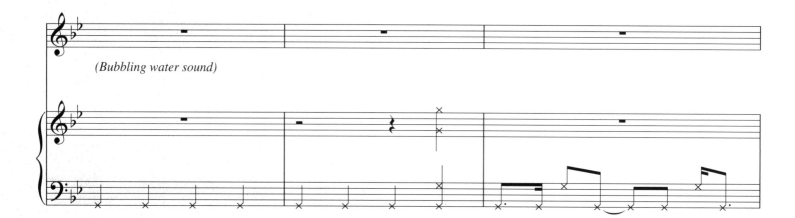

Dm7

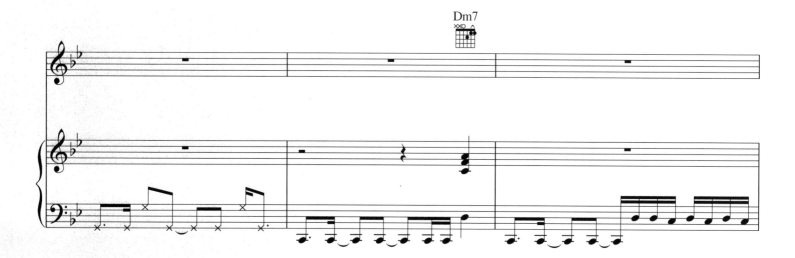

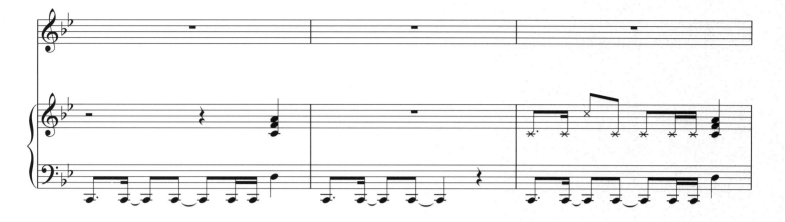

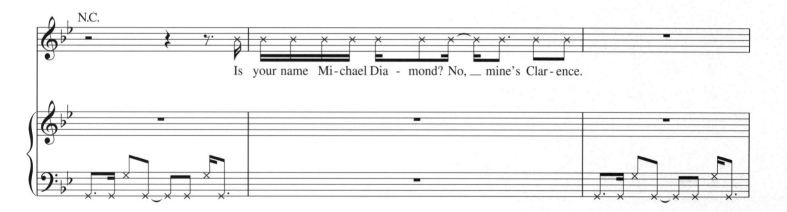

Is your name Mi-chael Dia - mond? No, __ mine's Clar-ence.

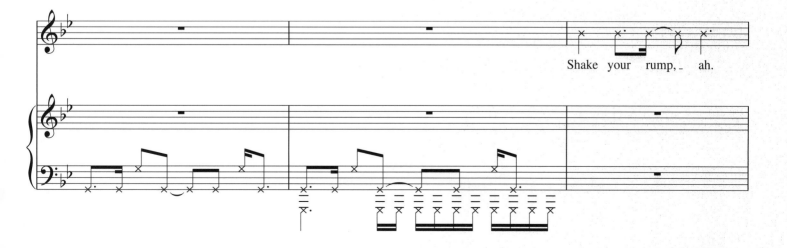

Shake your rump, __ ah.

(Loud cheering and screaming)

(End cheering and screaming)

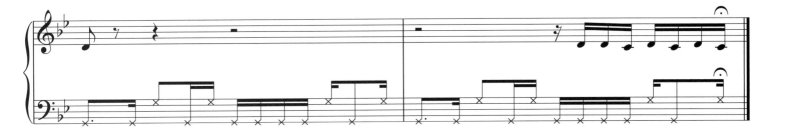

Rap Lyrics

Rap 1: Now I rock a house party at the drop of a hat. Yeah, I beat a biter down with a load on my back.
A lot of people they be jonesin' just to hear me rock the mic. They be starin' at the radio, stayin' up all night.
So like a pimp, I'm pimpin'. I got a boat to eat shrimp in. Nothin' wrong with my leg. I'm just B-Boy limpin'.
Got arrested at the Mardi Gras for jumpin' on a float. My man MCA's got a beard like a billy goat.
Oowah, oowah is my disco call. MCA, uh - huh, I'm gettin' roped y'all.
Routines I bust and the rhymes that I write, well, I'll be bustin' routines and rhymes all night.
Like eatin' burgers and chicken and you'll be pickin' your nose and I'm on time, homie, that's how it goes.
You heard my style, I think you missed the point. It's the joint.

Rap 2: Mike D., yeah? With your bad self runnin' things, what's up with your bad breath, onion rings?
Well, I'm Mike D. and I'm back from the dead, chillin' at the beach down at Club Med.
Make another record 'cause the people they want more of this.
Suckers, they be sayin' they can take out Adam Horovitz. Hurricane got clout.
Other DJ's, he'll put your head out. A puppet on a string, I'm paid to sing or rhyme.
I do my thing. I'm in a lava lamp inside my brain hotel. I might be freakin' or peakin' but I rock well.
The Patty Duke or the wrench and then I bust the tango. Got more rhymes than Jamaica got Mango Kangols.
I got the peg leg at the end of my stump, ah. Shake your rump, ah.

Rap 3: A full clout y'all. A full clout y'all. And when the mic is in my mouth I turn it out y'all. A full clout.
Never been dumped 'cause I'm the most mackinest. Never been jumped 'cause I'm known the most packinest.
Yeah, we got beef chief. We're knockin' out teeth chief and if you don't believe us you should question your belief chief.
I'm like Sam the butcher bringin' Alice the meat. Like Fred Flintstone drivin' around with bald feet.
Should I have another sip? Nah, skip it. In the back of the ride and bust with the whippet.
Rope a dope dookies all around the neck. Woo - ha, I got them all in check.
Runnin' from the law and the press and the parents. Is your name Michael Diamond? No, mine's Clarence.
From downtown Manhattan, the village. My style is wild and you know that it still is.
Disco bag schleppin' and you're doin' the bump, shake your rump, ah.

INTERGALACTIC

Words and Music by MICHAEL DIAMOND, ADAM YAUCH,
ADAM HOROVITZ and MARIO CALDATO JR.

Moderately

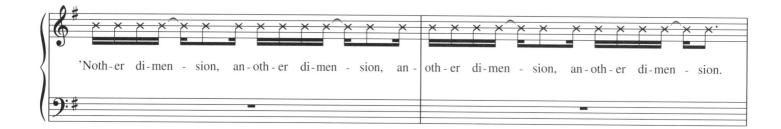

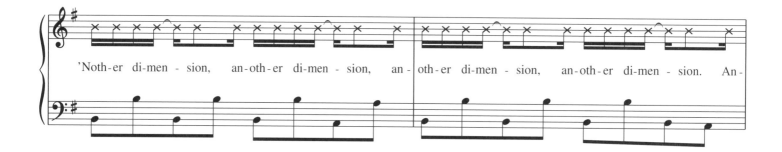

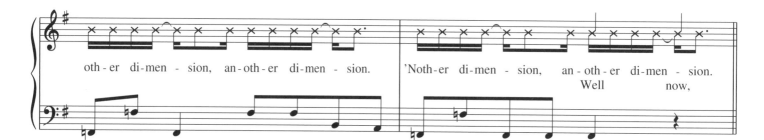

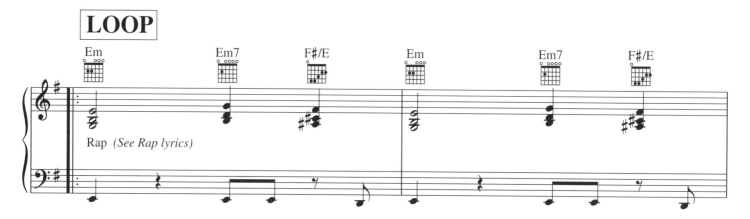

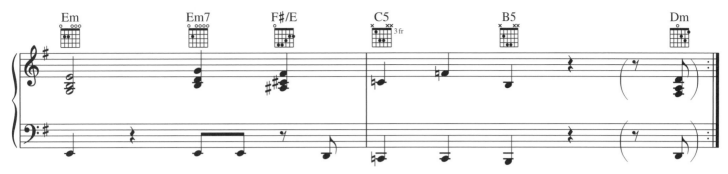

BRIDGE 1

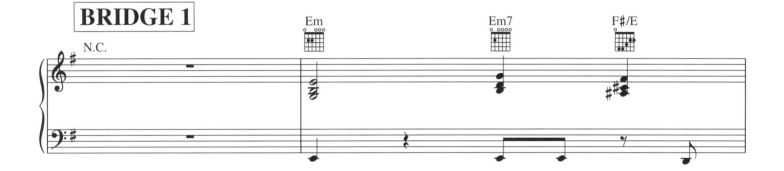

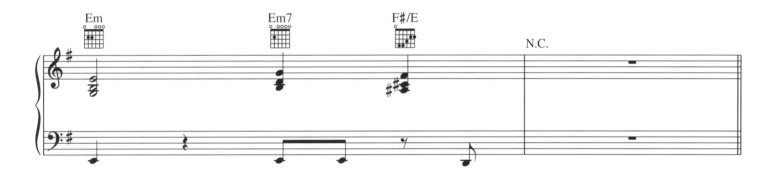

CHORUS

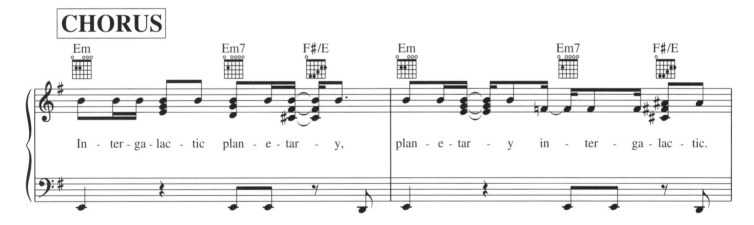

In - ter - ga - lac - tic plan - e - tar - y, plan - e - tar - y in - ter - ga - lac - tic.

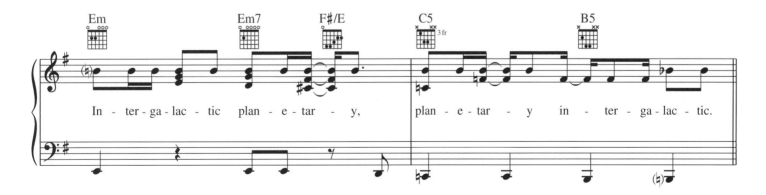

In - ter - ga - lac - tic plan - e - tar - y, plan - e - tar - y in - ter - ga - lac - tic.

BRIDGE 2

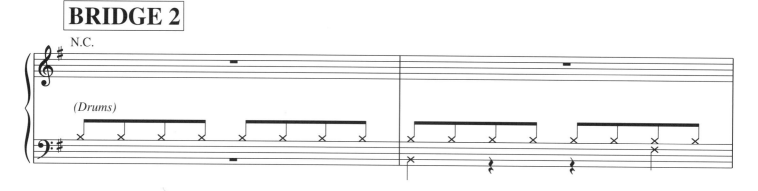

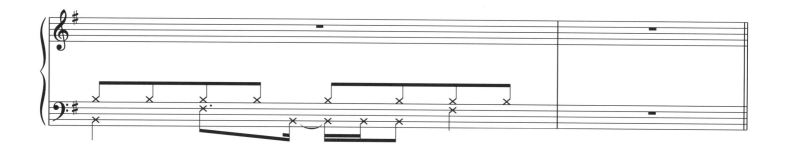

BRIDGE 3

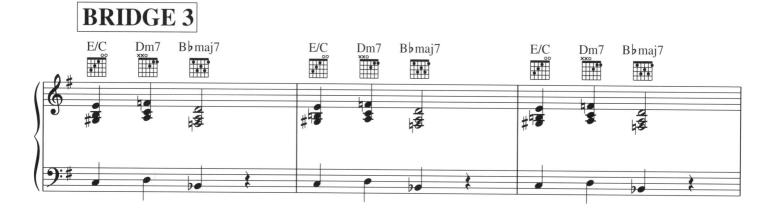

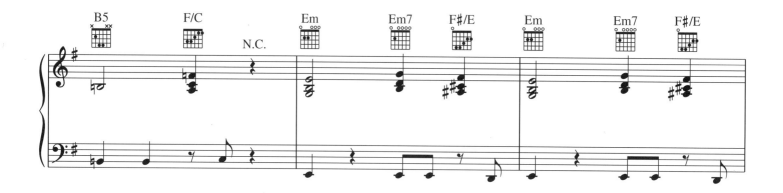

VERSE

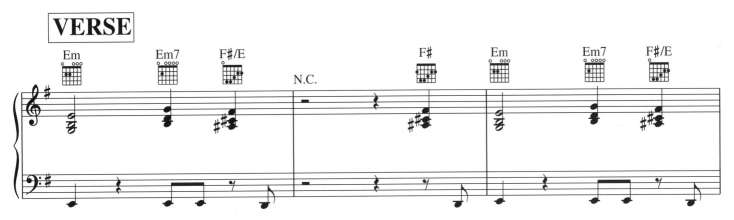

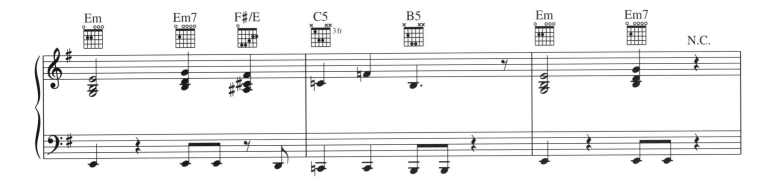

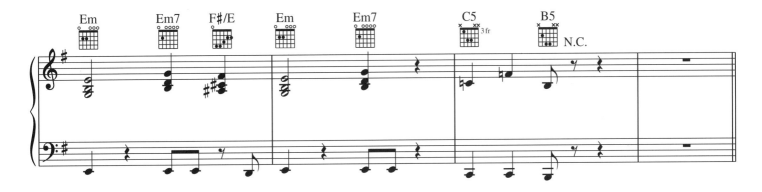

BRIDGE 4

ENDING

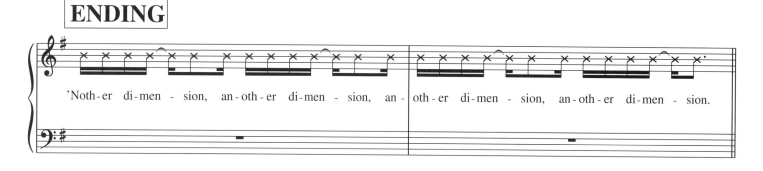

'Noth-er di-men - sion, an-oth-er di-men - sion, an - oth - er di-men - sion, an-oth-er di-men - sion.

Play 3 times

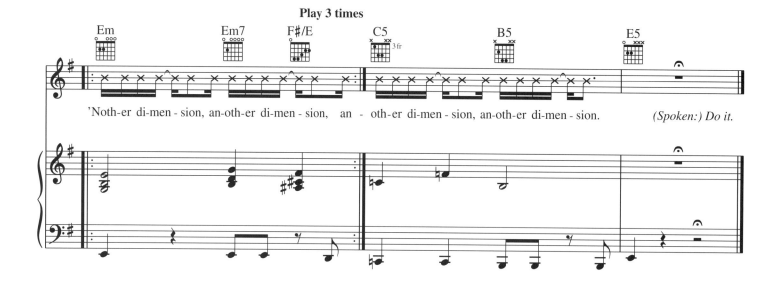

'Noth-er di-men - sion, an-oth-er di-men - sion, an - oth-er di-men - sion, an-oth-er di-men - sion.

(Spoken:) Do it.

Rap Lyrics

Intro: Intergalactic planetary, planetary intergalactic. *(4x)*

Another dimension. *(12x)*

Loop: Well now, don't you tell me to smile.
You stick around, I'll make it worth your while.
Got numbers beyond what you can dial.
Maybe it's because I'm so versatile.
Style, profile. I said it
Always brings me back when I hear Ooh Child.
From the Hudson River out to the Nile
I run the marathon to the very last mile.
Well, if you battle me I will revile.
People always saying my style is wild.
You've got gall, you've got guile.
Step to me, I'm a rapophile.

Bridge 1: If you want to battle you're in denial.
Coming from Uranus to check my style.
Go ahead, put my rhymes on trial.
Cast you off into exile.

Chorus: Intergalactic planetary, planetary intergalactic. *(2x)*

Bridge 2:   Jazz and Awol, that's our team.
Step inside the party, disrupt the whole scene.
When it comes to beats, well I'm a fiend.
I like my sugar with coffee and cream.

Loop: Well, I got to keep it going, keep it going full steam,
Too sweet to be sour, too nice to be mean.
Well, on the tough guy style I'm not too keen.
Try to change the world, I will plot and scheme.

Bridge 3:   Mario C likes to keep it clean (clean).
Gonna shine like a sunbeam (beam).
Keep on rapping 'cause that's my dream (dream).
Got an A from Moe Dee for sticking to themes.
Now, when it comes to envy y'all is green.
Jealous of the rhyme and the rhyme routine.
Another dimension, new galaxy.
Intergalactic planetary.

Chorus: Intergalactic planetary, planetary intergalactic. *(4x)*

Verse: We're from the family tree of old school hip-hip.
Kick off your shoes and relax your socks.
The rhymes will spread just like a pox
'Cause the music is live like an electric shock.
I am known to do the Wop (Wop),
Also known for the Flintstone Flop (Flop).
Tammy D gettin' biz on the crop.
Beastie Boys known to let the beat, mmm, drop.

Bridge 4:   Now, when I wrote graffiti my name was Slop.
If my rap's soup my beats is stock.
Step from the table when I start to drop.
I'm a lumberjack, DJ Adrock.
If you try to knock me you'll get mocked.
I'll stir-fry you in my wok.
Your knees'll start shaking and your fingers pop.
Like a pinch on the neck of Mr. Spock.

Chorus: Intergalactic planetary, planetary intergalactic. *(4x)*

Ending: Another dimension. *(12x)*
Do it.

SURE SHOT

Words and Music by MICHAEL DIAMOND,
ADAM YAUCH, ADAM HOROVITZ, MARIO CALDATO, JR.,
WENDELL FITE and JEREMY STEIG

Moderate groove

REFRAIN 1: *(See Rap lyrics)*

VERSE 1

(Drums)

*Recorded a half step lower.

Play 4 times

REFRAIN 2

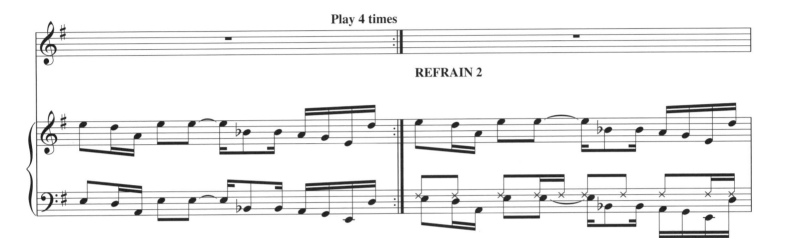

VERSE 2

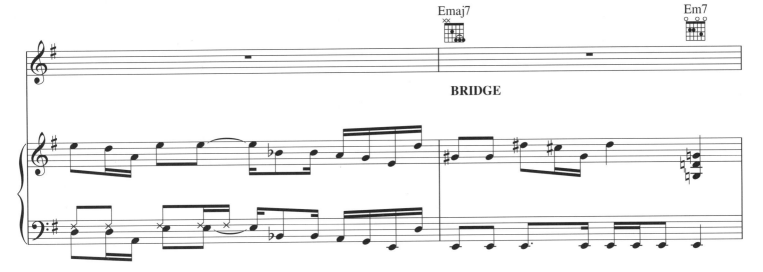

BRIDGE

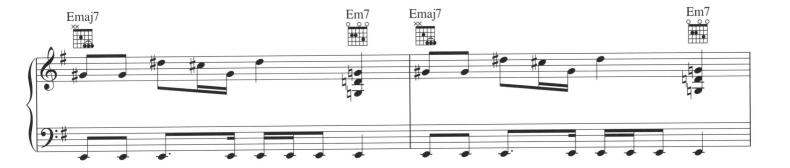

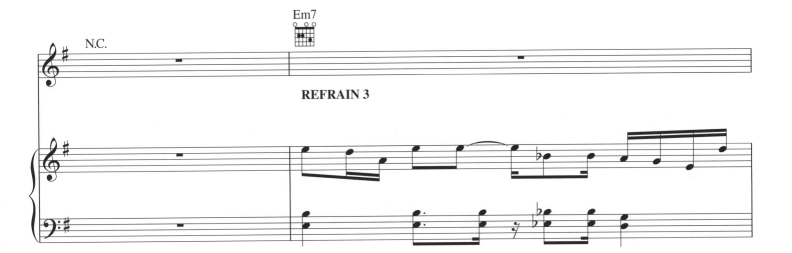

REFRAIN 3

VERSE 3

Play 3 times

Play 3 times

N.C.

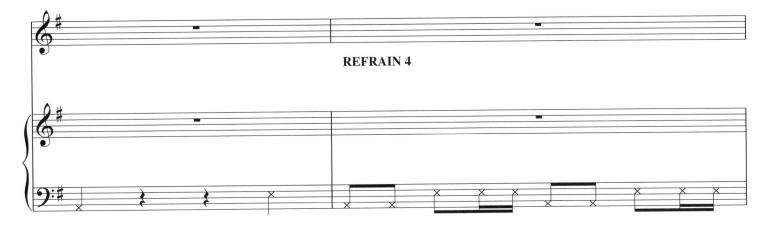

REFRAIN 4

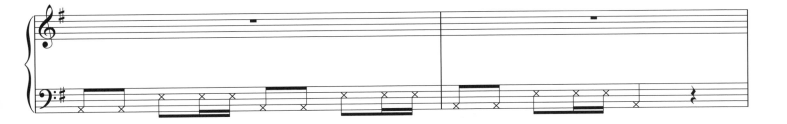

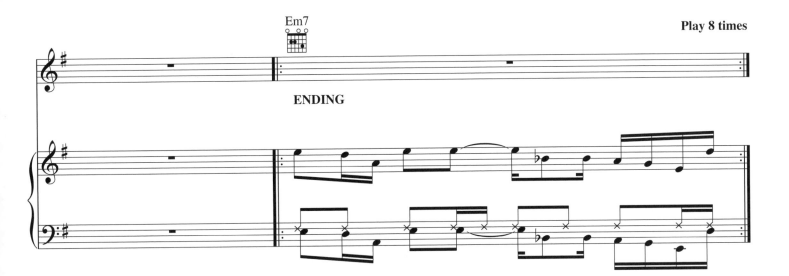

Em7

Play 8 times

ENDING

Rap Lyrics

Refrain 1:   'Cause you can't, you won't and you don't stop.
Because you can't, you won't and you don't stop.
A-well you can't, you won't and you don't stop.
Mike D. come and rock the sure shot.

Verse 1:   I got the brand-new doo doo, guaranteed like Yoo-hoo.
I'm on like Dr. John, yeah, Mr. Zu Zu.
I'm a newlywed, I'm not a divorcé,
And everything I do is funky like Lee Dorsey.
Well, it's the takin' of the Pelham One, Two, Three.
If you want a doo doo rhyme, then come see me.
I've got the savoir faire with the unique rhyme and I keep it on and on.
It's never quittin' time and strictly hand-held is the style I go.
Never rock the mic with the pantyhose.
I strap on my ear goggles and I'm ready to go,
'Cause at the boards is the man they call Mario.
Pull up at the function and you know I'm Kojak to all the party people that are on my botak.
I've got more action than my man John Woo,
And I got mad hits like I was Rod Carew.

Refrain 2:   Yeah, because you can't, you won't and you don't stop.
Because you can't, you won't and you don't stop.
You know you can't, you won't and you don't stop.
Adrock come and rock the sure shot.

Verse 2:   Brother, brother, cane will cross fade on your ass and bust your ear drums.
Now, listen ev'rybody 'cause I'm shiftin' gears.
I'm fresh like Dougie when I get my specs in.
On the microphone I come correct,
Timin' like a clock when I rock the hip hop.
Top-notch is my stock on the soapbox.
I got more rhymes than I got grey hairs and that's a lot because I got my share.
I got a hole in my head and there's no one to fix it.
Gotta straighten my thoughts. I'm thinkin' too much sick shit.
Everyone just takes and takes, takes, takes, takes.
Allow me to step back, I gotta contemplate.
Well, I'm like Lee Perry, I'm very on rock the microphone and then I'm gone.
I'm like Vaughn bode. I'm a Cheech wizard. Never quittin', so won't you listen.

Bridge: Ah, ah.
Ah, ah, ah.
Ah, yes indeed, it's fun time, fun time.

Refrain 3:   Because you can't, you won't and you don't stop.
Because you can't, you won't and you don't stop.
A-well you can't, you won't and you don't stop.
M.C.A. come and rock the sure shot.

Verse 3:   I want to say a little somethin' that's long overdue.
The disrespect to women has got to be through.
To all the mothers and the sisters and the wives and friends, I want to offer my love and respect to the end.
Well, you say I'm twenty somethin' and I shouldn't be slackin' but I'm workin' harder than ever
And you could call it mackin'.
So I'm supposed to sit upon the couch and watchin' my TV.
Still listenin' to wax, I'm not usin' the CD.
Well, I'm that kid in the corner all fucked up and I wanna so I'm gonna
Take a piece of the pie. Why not, I'm not quittin'.
Think I'm gon' change up my style just to fit in.
I keep my underwear up with a piece of elastic.
I use a bullshit mic that's made out of plastic to send my rhymes out to all the nations.
Like Ma Bell, I got the ill communication.

Refrain 4:   Because you can't, you won't and you don't stop.
Because you can't, you won't and you don't stop.
A-well you can't, you won't and you don't stop.
Born and they're rockin' the sure shot.

Ending: B-boys, B-girls.

BODY MOVIN'

Words and Music by BEASTIE BOYS,
MARIO CALDATO, JR. and TITO PUENTE

Moderate beat

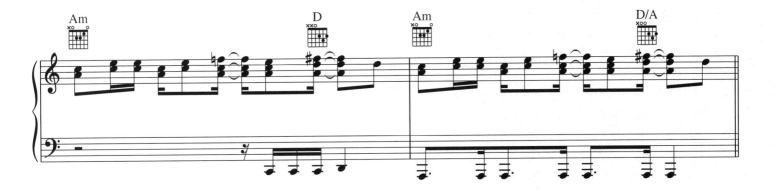

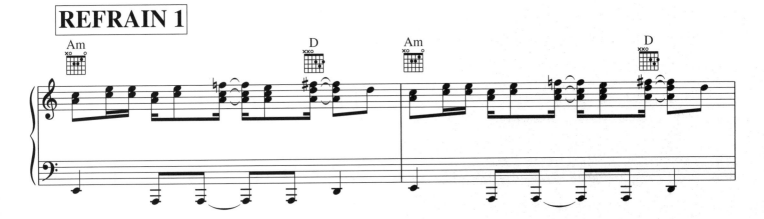

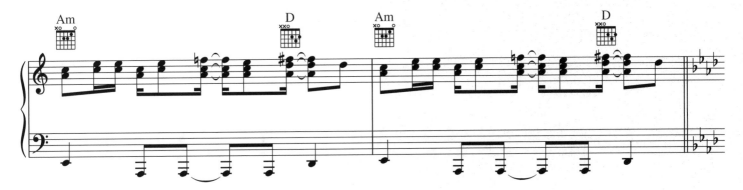

LOOP 1

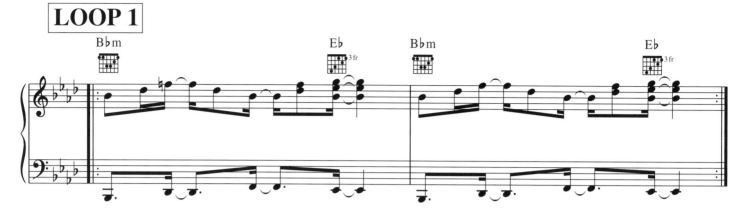

BRIDGE 1 **REFRAIN 2**

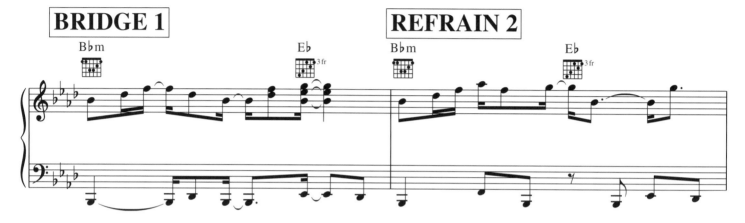

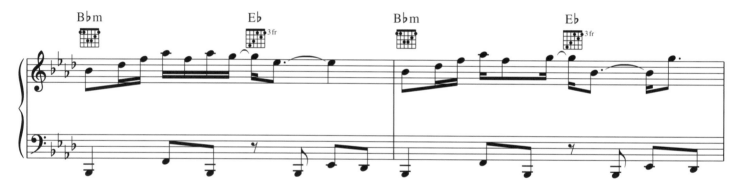

BRIDGE 2

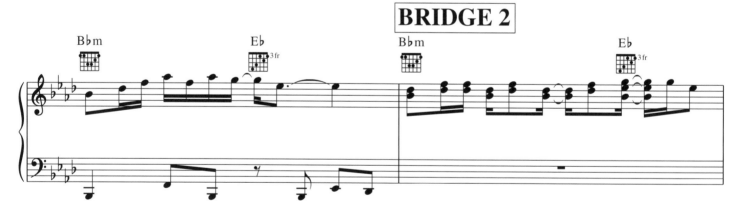

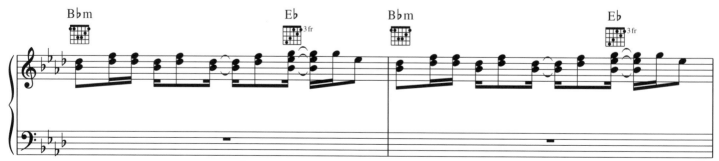

LOOP 2

REFRAIN 3

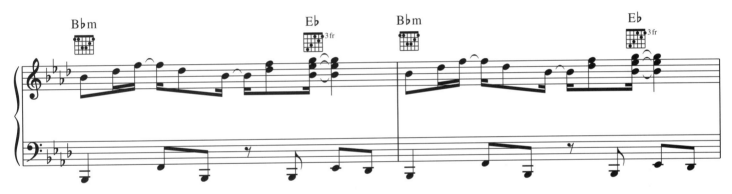

BRIDGE 3

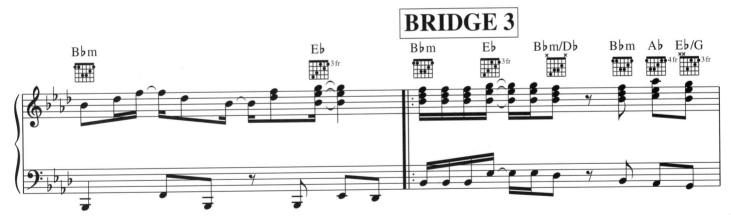

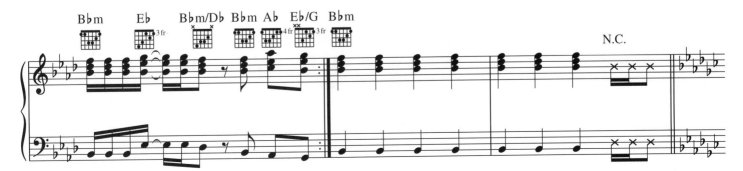

LOOP 3

BRIDGE 4

ENDING

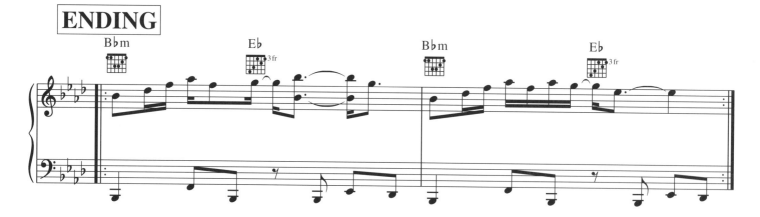

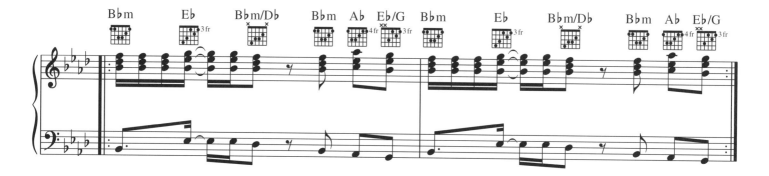

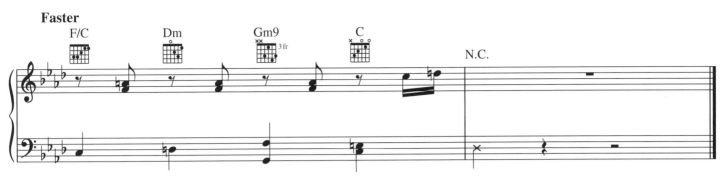

LYRICS

Intro: Ready, one.
You will do this four times with the left, four with the right,
Then eight times with both, then repeat.

Refrain 1: Body movin', body movin',
A 1 sound and the sound so soothing.
Body movin', body movin',
We be getting down and you know we're crush groovin'.

Loop 1: Now, let me get some action from the back section.
We need body rocking, not perfection.
Let your backbone flip, but don't slip a disc,
And let your spine unwind, just take a risk.
I wanna do the freak until the break of dawn.
Tell me, party people, is that so wrong?
The ship is docking, interlocking,
And uprocking electroshocking.
We're getting down computer action.
Do the robotic satisfaction.
All of y'all, get off the wall.

Bridge 1: Have a ball and get involved with...

Refrain 2: Body movin', body movin' (stand erect),
A 1 sound and the sound so soothing (arms down),
Body movin', body movin' (swing left arm big),
We be getting down and you know we're crush groovin' (same with the right).

Bridge 2:   Flame on, I'm gone.
I'm so sweet, like a nice bon-bon.
Came out rapping when I was born.
Mom said rock it 'til the break of dawn.

Loop 2:   Puttin' bodies in motion 'cause I got the notion,
Like Roy Cormier with the coconut lotion.
The sound of music makin' you insane.
You can't explain to people this type of mindframe.
And like a bottle of Chateau Neuf Du Pap,
I'm fine like wine when I start to rap.
We need body rocking, not perfection.
Let me get some action from the back section.

Refrain 3:   Body movin', body movin',
A 1 sound and the sound so soothing.
Body movin', body movin',
We be getting down and you know we're crush groovin'.

Bridge 3:   Left arm ready and...

Loop 3:   One, and again, stand erect.
Mike D with the master plan.
I said ooh, my my and thank you, ma'am.
And when I grab the mic, you scream, "Ooh, goddamn."
The crème de la crème is who I am.
MCA, where have you been?
Packed like sardines in the tin.

Bridge 4:   So kick off your shoes and put on your swim fins
'Cause when it comes to quarries I'm known to swim.
And adrock, light up the place,
And if you pull my card you pull the ace.
And if you ask me turn up the bass,
And if you play Defender, I could be your hyperspace.

Refrain 3:   Body movin', body movin',
A 1 sound, sound so soothing.
Body movin', body movin',
We be getting down and you know we're crush groovin'.

Ending: You will do eight hops on the left, eight on the right.
Four left, four right, two left, two right.
Then one each left, right, left, right.
Start and land on the balls of the feet.
Left foot, ready, it's one, two, three, four, five.

TRIPLE TROUBLE

Words and Music by MICHAEL DIAMOND,
ADAM HOROVITZ, ADAM YAUCH,
NILE RODGERS and BERNARD EDWARDS

Heavy groove

Refrain 1: *(See Rap lyrics)*

Rap 1

(Percussion)

Refrain 2

(Percussion)

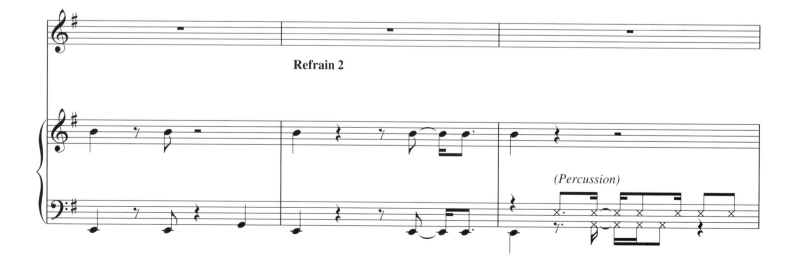

Rap 2

(Percussion)

Refrain 3

Bridge

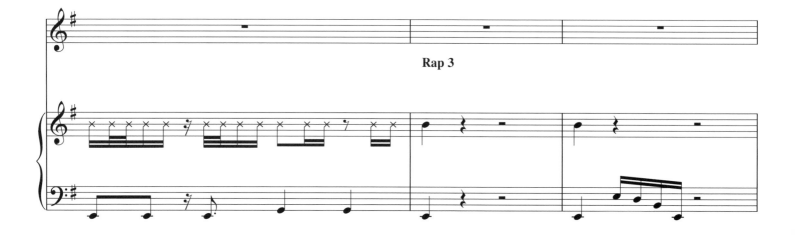

Rap 3

N.C.

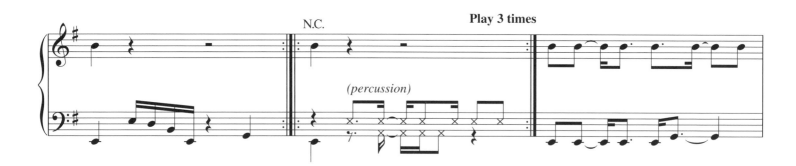

N.C. **Play 3 times**

(percussion)

Refrain 4

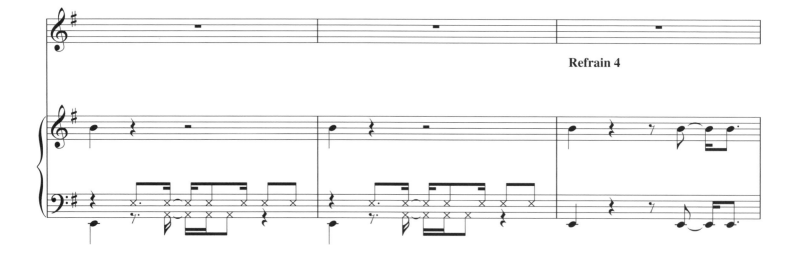

Rap Lyrics

Refrain 1: If you, if you, wanna know, wanna know the real deal about the three, well, let me tell you we're triple trouble, y'all.
We're gonna bring you up to speed. Check it out.

Rap 1: 'Cause I'm a specializer rhyme reviser. Ain't sellin' out to advertisers.
What you get is what you see and you won't see me in the advertisin'. See, I like to party, not drink Bacardi,
'Cause I'm not lookin' to throw up on nobody. Known for my spiel, a wheelie one wheel. This is like havin' a delicious meal.
And well, movin' the crowd, well, that's a must. I got some words that apply to us,
And that's mesmerizin', tantalizin', captivatin'. We're devastatin'.

Refrain 2: If you, if you, wanna know, wanna know the real deal about the three, well, let us tell you we're triple trouble, y'all.
We got to bring you up to speed. Now check it out.

Rap 2: Here's one for the bleachers and the upper tier. Versatile, All-Temp-A-Cheer. If you want a drink call Mr. Belvedere.
Run this rap game like a brigadier. I got kicks on the one, seven and eleven, snares on the five and thirteen.
Rhymes on time and that's the given. We're hot on the disco scene. Check it, check it.
Slow down with the army, got to stop stingin'. Source of the problem's at the origin.
You got lyrics that have got me cringin'. You're like a fish, why quit your damn whingin'.

Refrain 3: If you, if you, wanna know, wanna know the real deal about the three, well, let me tell you we're triple trouble, y'all.
We're gonna bring you up to speed, so check it out.

Rap 3: Bam, super nature goddamn. Cerrone on the microphone I am. Adrock, A.K.A. sharp cheddar, my rhymes are better.
What the Helen of Troy is that? Did I hear you say my rhymes is whack? I'm beautiful, you can't touch me.
If you pick a rose, well, you might just bleed. We're originators. You can't feign ignorance or pass the blame.
'Nuff rhymes comin' out the brain. 'Nuff beats to drive you insane. 'Nuff moves to make your neck crane.
'Nuff skills to make the rhymes ingrain. 'Nuff heat to leave you in flames. 'Nuff style that you can't defame.
You see, I walk like Jabba the Hutt with style so new y'all be like, what? Turn this party out like a bon vivant with the
Skill at will that I know you want. On a hot day with a iced latte. Devious like Wile E. Coyote.
Hot to trotte or maybe notte, 'cause little did they know there was a baby in her body.
We're mesmerizin', tantalizin', captivatin' and devastatin'.

Refrain 4: If you, if you, wanna know, wanna know the real deal about the three, well, let me tell you we're triple trouble, y'all.
We're gonna bring you up to speed. Check it out.

SABOTAGE

Words and Music by MICHAEL DIAMOND,
ADAM YAUCH and ADAM HOROVITZ

Fast Hard Rock

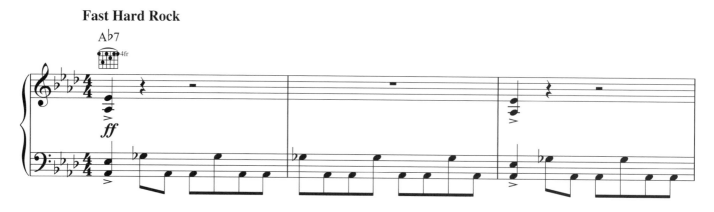

Rap 1: *(See Rap lyrics)*

Rap 4

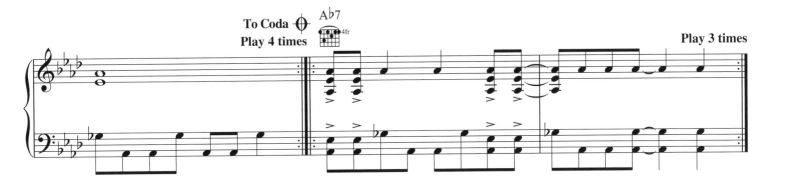

To Coda ⊕ A♭7
Play 4 times

Play 3 times

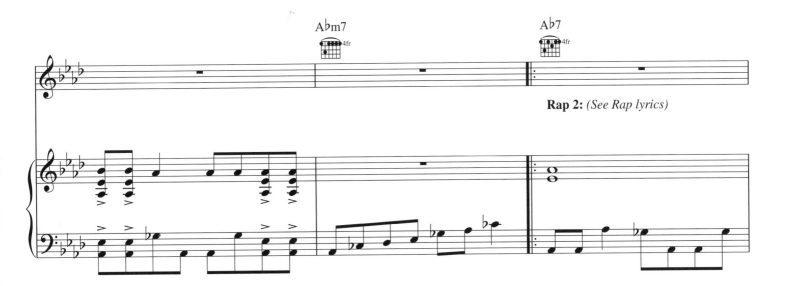

A♭m7

A♭7

Rap 2: *(See Rap lyrics)*

Play 2 times

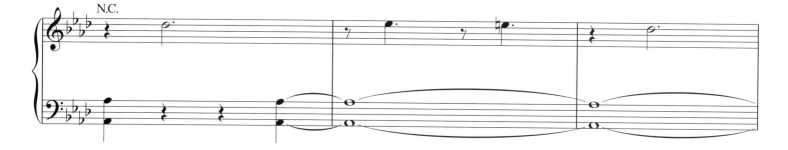

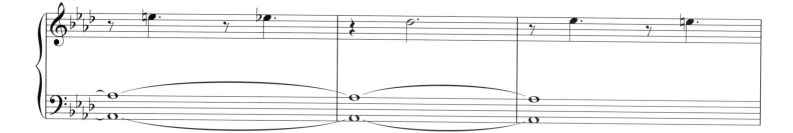

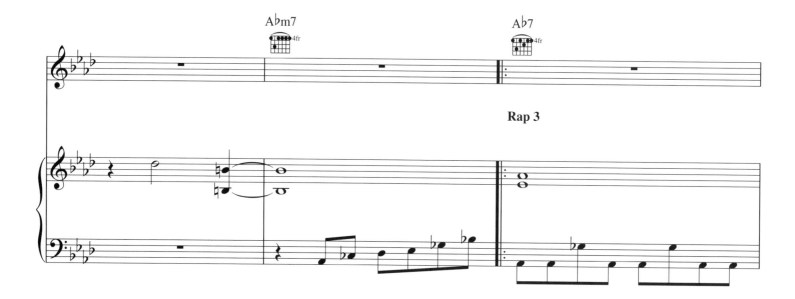

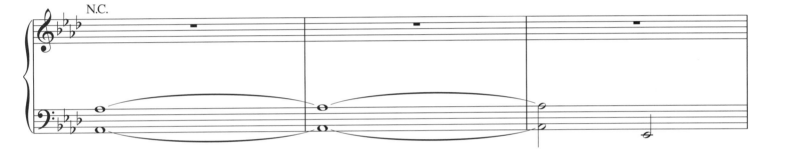

Rap Lyrics

Rap 1:   I can't stand it. I know you planned it. I'm gon' set it straight, this Watergate.
                  I can't stand rockin' when I'm in here 'cause your crystal ball ain't so crystal clear.
                  So, while you sit back and wonder why, I got this fuckin' thorn in my side.
                  Oh my God, it's a mirage. I'm tellin' y'all it's sabotage.

Rap 2:   So, so, so listen up 'cause you can't say nothin'. You shut me down with a push of your button.
                  Betcha I'm out and I'm gone. I'll tell you now I keep it on and on.

Rap 3:   'Cause what you see you might not get, and we can bet so don't you get souped yet.
                  Schemin' on a thing that's a mirage. I'm tryin' to tell you now it's sabotage.

Rap 4:   I can't stand it. I know you planned it. I'm gon' set it straight, this Watergate.
                  But I can't stand rockin' when I'm in this place because I feel disgrace because you're all in my face.
                  But make no mistakes and switch up my channel. I'm Buddy Rich when I fly off the handle.
                  What could it be, it's a mirage. You're schemin' on a thing that's sabotage.

FIGHT FOR YOUR RIGHT
(To Party)

Words and Music by RICK RUBIN,
ADAM HOROVITZ and ADAM YAUCH

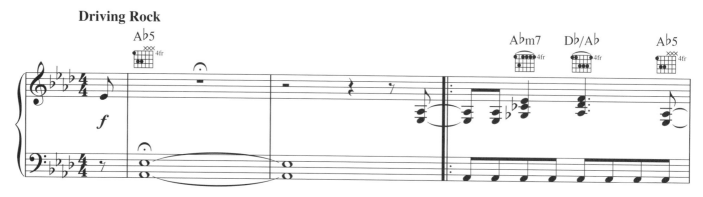

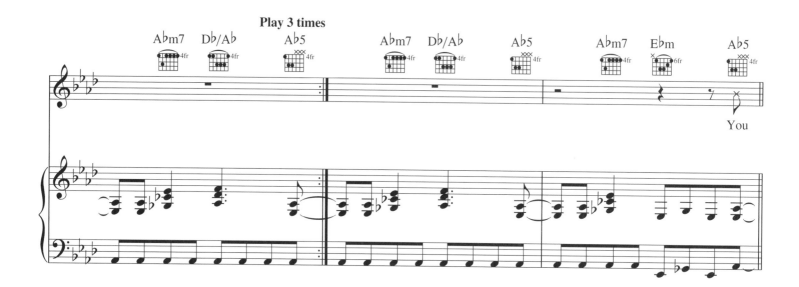

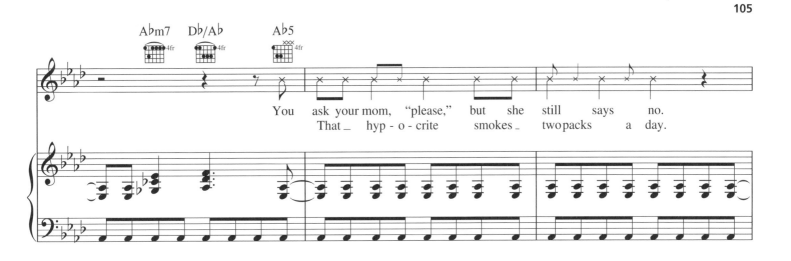

You ask your mom, "please," but she still says no.
That hyp-o-crite smokes two packs a day.

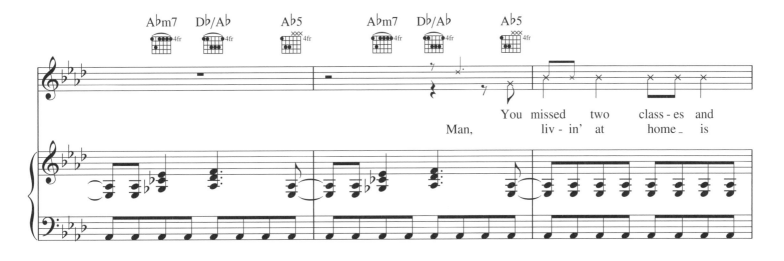

Man, You missed two class-es and liv-in' at home is

no home-work, such a drag. Now but your

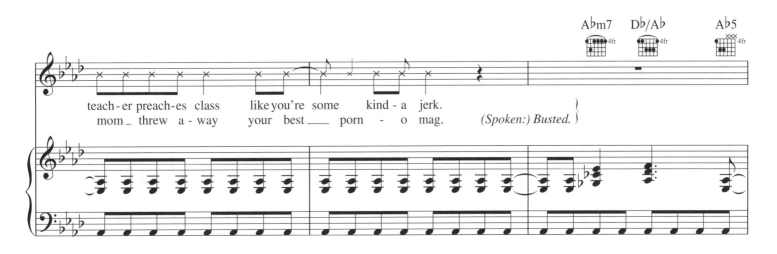

teach-er preach-es class like you're some kind-a jerk.
mom threw a-way your best porn-o mag. (Spoken:) Busted.

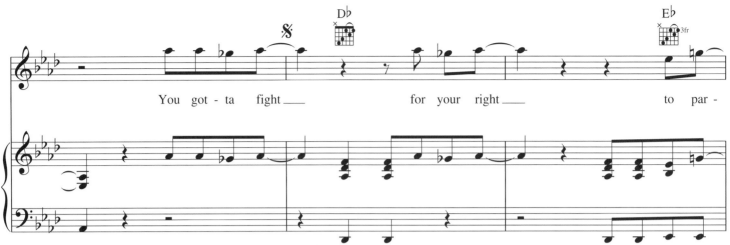

You got - ta fight ____ for your right ____ to par -

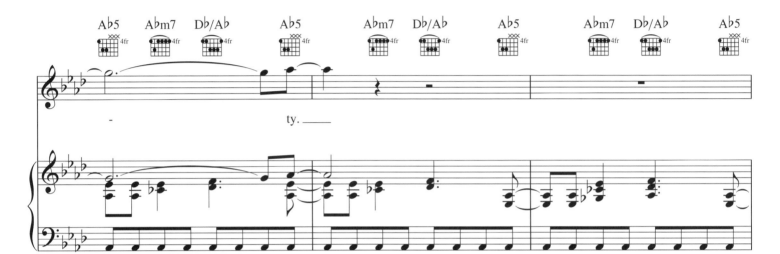

- ty. ____

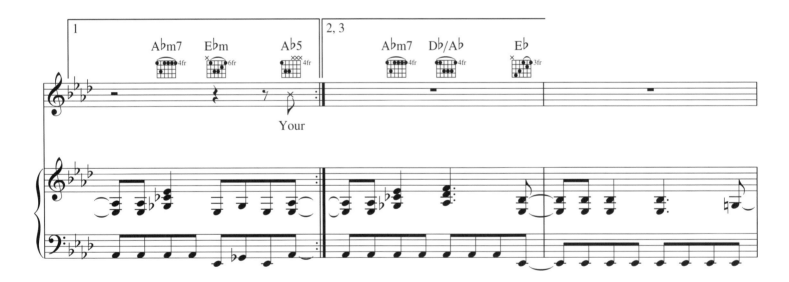

Your

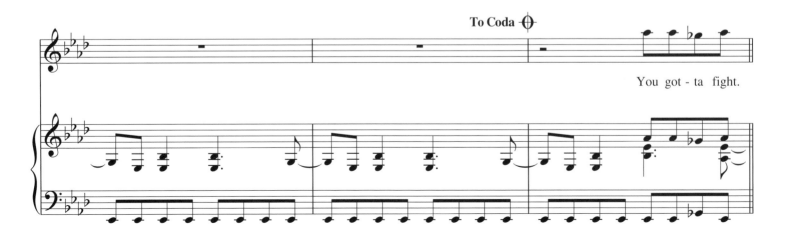

You got - ta fight.

Play 3 times

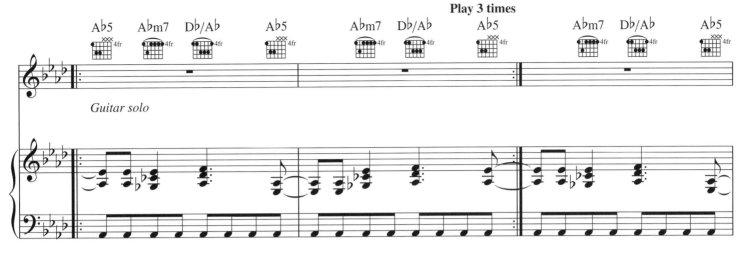

Guitar solo

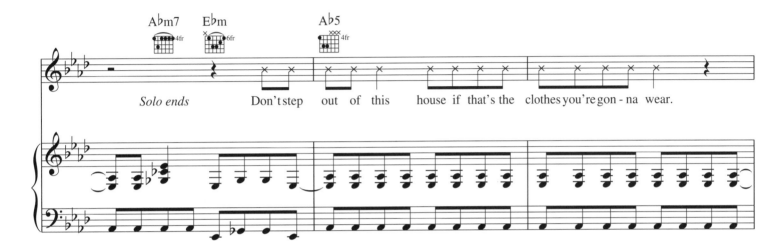

Solo ends Don't step out of this house if that's the clothes you're gon - na wear.

I'll kick you out of my home if you don't

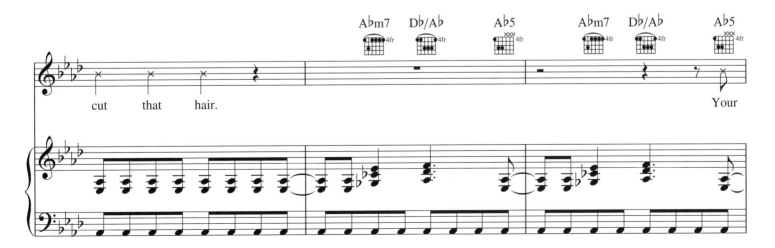

cut that hair. Your